THE WELL-TROD STAGE

The well-trod stage of The Kenton Theatre Henley-on-Thames

Bill Port

THE WELL-TROD STAGE

The well-trod stage of The Kenton Theatre Henley-on-Thames

First published by Robinswood Press 2005.

© Bill Port 2005

The Kenton Theatre (Henley-on-Thames) Management Society Ltd retains copyright in all materials belonging to it which are reproduced here with its permission.

Bill Port has asserted his rights under the Copyright, Designs and Patents Act 1988 to be identified as the author of this work.

Cover design by Lorraine Payne. Cover illustrations by JMW Turner © National Maritime Museum, London (BHC0565) and George Marshall. Design and layout by Steve Emms. Edited by Roy Lett. Printed by Latimer Trend, Plymouth.

All rights reserved. No part of this publication may be reproduced, stored in a retrieval system or transmitted in any form, or by any means, electronic, mechanical, photocopying, recording or otherwise, without prior permission in writing from the publisher.

Robinswood Press   South Avenue   Stourbridge   United Kingdom

Robinswood Press

Stourbridge England   Dublin Republic of Ireland
www.robinswoodpress.com

ISBN 1-869981-847

Contents

Acknowledgements iv
About the Author v
Foreword vii
A message from Kate Winslet viii
"The Matter is Decided, Mr Dee." 1
Our ends by our beginnings know 3
"The finest scene imaginable." 7
Billingsgate, Cripplegate, Newgate and Hellgate 9
The New and Elegant Theatre 13
From Thomas Morton to a pint pot of ale 17
Limelight, blackboards and pews 21
For details see small bills 25
No more Pleasant Sunday Afternoons 29
Twice nightly – very poor houses 33
Support your local theatre 39
A small group of local residents 47
"This misery which is called a theatre." 55
"I have sensed the spirit of a lady." 73
A place of its own 77
A very successful decade 81
A far-sighted scheme 85
Entirely due to the people of Henley 89
Appendices 95

Acknowledgments

THE WELL-TROD STAGE has been produced with the co-operation and authorisation of the Board of The Kenton Theatre (Henley-on-Thames) Management Society Ltd, of which the author is a member, although the Society is not responsible for its content or publication. The author wishes to thank those who have given him photographs and programmes to assist his research and to express his gratitude to the many individuals whose knowledge and friendship have helped to bring this publication to fruition, especially Bob Brackston, Georg and Wendy Briner, the late Dorothy Clark, Cliff Colborne, Nansi Diamond, Peter Frankenburg, the late Don Hookins, Roger Kendal, Kate Lindsey, John and Ann Luker, the late Joan Morgan, Jennifer Scott, Teddy Selwyn, Francis Shepherd, Nikki Stanton, the late Molly Sugden, Jean Sutherland, David Tapp, Margot Thomas, John and Judy Yeates, and the staff of The Henley Library, The Henley Standard, and The River and Rowing Museum.

About the Author

Bill Port was born in Lanark in 1931 where he made his stage début at the age of five. He made regular appearances in the Gilbert and Sullivan Operas and Shakespeare plays staged by Dalziel High School in Motherwell where he was a pupil. After growing up in the usual way he moved to London in 1951 and began a career in the laundry industry, eventually taking control of all the laundries owned by British Rail.

He renewed his amateur acting career when, with his wife Pat and their two children, he moved to Peppard, near Henley-on-Thames. Bill and Pat joined the Chiltern Edge Players, later becoming members of the Henley Players and the Henley Amateur Operatic and Dramatic Society which performed at The Kenton Theatre. First Pat, then Bill, joined the management society of the Theatre and were subsequently elected to the Board of Directors.

With his long involvement, Bill came to realise the huge significance of the many individuals who, throughout the Theatre's life and right into the present, had worked so hard – generally with little acknowledgement – to maintain the presence of this precious facility at the heart of Henley. The bi-centenary of The Kenton Theatre seemed to Bill an appropriate moment to put right this omission and to record the ups and downs of England's fourth oldest theatre.

This book is dedicated to Pat.

New Street, Henley-on-Thames, about the turn of the century. The setting for our story. The theatre building is the third on the left.

© George Marshall 2005

Foreword by Boris Johnson MP

When the Romans brought civilisation to Britain and the rest of Western Europe, they brought with them a certain set of identical amenities.

There were the baths. There was the forum. There were the latrines. There was the race track. Above all, there was the theatre.

It is a proof of Henley's position at the acme of British civilisation that a town of barely more than 10,000 inhabitants should now have a fabulous pedestrianised forum, a bath in every house (more or less), some distinguished latrines in the Greys Road car park, the world's premier aquatic race track and the fourth-oldest theatre in the country. It is a wonderful institution, and I hope you will enjoy this excellent history.

Boris Johnson
MP for Henley-on-Thames

A message from Kate Winslet

I remember my experiences at The Kenton Theatre so well, and with such great affection. I did several productions at the Kenton, including *Adrian Mole.* There was nothing as exciting as the backstage chatter, the cramped dressing rooms where everyone claimed their own little patch of dressing table and decorated the mirrors with lipstick and eyeliner, the dusty smell of hired costumes and the scent of hairspray.

What fun we had!

Kate Winslet

"The matter is decided, Mr Dee."

On 20th January 1904, the Mayor of Henley, Alderman Charles Clements, called the monthly and quarterly meeting of the Town Council to order. He glanced round while the Town Clerk, Mr JF Cooper, noted the names of the members who were present and read apologies from the others. The Mayor read out the minutes of the committee meeting which had been held at St Mary's Hall on 14th January and which had been attended by ten members of the Council. He moved that the minutes be adopted and added that there was just one other thing which he would like to refer to, namely the question of the name 'St Mary's Hall'. He said that, although the name was suitable enough when the Hall was used solely for Church purposes, he felt it was not appropriate now that the Hall was being used as a theatre and for entertainments. He had spoken with the Charity Trustees that morning and, while they agreed that it was a matter for the Corporation to decide, they had no objection to a change of name.

He suggested that the name should be altered to 'Kenton Hall' in order to associate it with the name of Robert Kenton who had, in 1632, bequeathed the property, which was then the town workhouse, to the Bridge Trust. In this way the Council would perpetuate the name of a benefactor to the town. He added that the Charity Trustees had approved the name and hoped that the Council would agree. He then moved that the name be altered to 'Kenton Hall'. Alderman Chamberlain seconded the motion.

There was some discussion as to whether the name should be 'Kenton's Hall' or 'Kenton Hall' and the Mayor pointed out that the name 'Kenton's Hall' would clash with the residence in White Hill which was known as 'Kenton's'.

Councillor Campion objected. *"The hall has been known as 'St Mary's Hall' for a long time,"* he said, *"and the public would be a long time before they would appreciate the change."*

Councillor Reeves supported the Mayor's proposition saying that the Church people had thought for a long time that the name should be altered.

The Mayor proceeded to take the vote when Councillor Dee interposed to say he would like to have a little more time to consider the matter. The Mayor replied, *"The matter is decided, Mr Dee. I am very sorry."*

And so St Mary's Hall, formerly The National School, The Congregational Hall and The New Theatre acquired, for the first time in its ninety-nine years, the name 'Kenton'. However, there were to be several more name changes before the words 'Kenton Theatre' appeared above the door.

Our ends by our beginnings know

History has no beginning and ends in the present, so it is almost a matter of luck where you start to research. You may travel a long way back in time and still not be sure that you have reached the true beginning. So, where does the story of The Kenton Theatre begin? Come back with me to 1485 – a most important year in the history of England. That year Henry Tudor defeated Richard III at the Battle of Bosworth Field on 22nd August and was crowned King Henry VII in Westminster Abbey on 30th October. So ended the rule of the Plantagenets; so also ended the Medieval Period and England moved into the times of the Tudors.

In Tudor times England began to change. The country became more prosperous and one of the things which people began to spend their extra wealth on was entertainment – especially dramatic performances.

The early Medieval theatre was largely frowned upon by the Church. Later, formal drama, which had almost disappeared with the fall of the Roman Empire, began to re-emerge but it was controlled by the Clergy. Short plays or *tropes* like the *Quem Quaeritis* consisted merely of a few lines exchanged between the Three Marys at an Easter service. Gradually these *tropes* became more common and were included in Christmas and other festivals and also as an adjunct to some religious processions. In time they developed into the *Mystery Plays* which had, of course, a strong religious theme. Later, *Mummers' Plays* became popular all over the country. With their central theme of death and revival they symbolised the resurrection although they were obviously based upon a pagan core originating at least as far back as 1000 B.C.

With the advent of the Tudors, plays became more secular. Henley seems to have been well to the forefront in performing them. In 1503 four plays were performed in Henley (either in front of St Mary's Church, the normal place for such performances, or in the open space now known as Broadgates, where the Stuart Turner building stands). The plays were *The Three Kings of Cologne, John Sharp, The Resurrection* and *Robyn Hode*. It seems that these plays, or some of them, were performed as part of the Hocktide celebrations and they made a profit.

It is worth stepping aside for a few moments to consider Hocktide. Dr Plott, the historian, tells us:

"Hocktide is agreed by all to be a festival celebrated in memory of the great slaughter of the Danes in the time of King Aethelred (the Unready), they being all slain throughout England in the one day, and in the great part, by women; whence it came to pass, that the women to this day bear the chief rule in this feast, stopping all passages with ropes and chains, and laying hold on passengers, and exacting some small matter from them, with part whereof they make merry, and part they dispose of to pious uses, such as reparation of their church etc."

It is unlikely that this slaughter of the Danes occurred on exactly the same day all over England. It was probably spread over a longer period. This may account for the variety of dates proposed. These vary from the second Tuesday after Easter, the 9th April or the 19th September (suggested by Julian Richards in his television programme about the Vikings). The year was 1001 or, according to some, 1002.

Mostly the celebration of Hocktide died out in the 16th Century when it became illegal to demand money, but even today it is celebrated, albeit in a different form, in some parts of the country including Hexham in Cumbria and Hungerford in Berkshire. No matter when or where they took place, the celebrations of Hocktide, in Henley at least, always involved the performance of plays.

The minutes of the Henley Corporation for the 14th year of the reign of Henry VII (1499) have an entry which says that it was

"agreed that the money remaining in the hands of the collectors of the play of Robyn Hode, *and in the hands of the women of Henley, for money collected at Hocktyde should be applied at the discretion of the Corporation for the buying of a thuribulum of silver, to be made against the Feast of All Souls next coming".*

Unfortunately, they did not manage to get enough money to buy the silver thuribulum (a kind of censer) in time for All Souls, but according to the Corporation minutes for 1503:

"the warden, churchmen and committee have settled with John Andrew Dyer [dyeing seems to have been his profession] for the purchase of a new silver-gilt censer which cost £7-8-9, 18/- of which came from the King Plays' money collected when his son Ric Andrew played the leading part..."

There was obviously some pride in being chosen to play the leading part in the play. John Andrew was also given money from the profits of other plays in order to pay the bill from the goldsmith.

On 30th September that same year John Andrew died and his will recorded several bequests. To his wife Agnes he left £4 and fourteen silver spoons. To William, his brother, he left eight silver spoons and his best gown. He made other bequests and finally he left

"to Robt Kenton, a tenement [property holding] in Henley for an obit to the value of 6/8".

He also appointed Robert Kenton to supervise his executors.

So here are the very early beginnings of The Kenton Theatre. First, the general interest in Henley in watching and performing in plays and then the acquisition by Robert Kenton of the property which his grandson was to leave in his will to the Henley Corporation 129 years later in 1632.

Diana Rigg

Rodney Bewes

"The finest scene imaginable."

The first purpose-built theatre in England was erected at Shoreditch in 1576 and was unimaginatively called 'The Theatre'. It was built in Shoreditch as the authorities in London refused to allow plays to be performed within the city because of the unsavoury reputation of the performers. Shakespeare's company built their theatre, 'The Globe', in Southwark in 1599 for the same reason. Despite the increase in the number of purpose-built theatres, plays continued to be performed in open spaces, the courtyards of inns or at the homes of the aristocracy who commissioned them for the entertainment of their guests. Writers or performers were able, in the secure atmosphere of a private house, to break away from the religious themes and to mount plays with more secular and down-to-earth subjects. The owner of the house, however, had to be careful what type of plays he permitted to be performed. Anything controversial or political might well lead to trouble.

Over the years, Henley became the home of a number of aristocrats and gentry who encouraged plays to be performed either in their homes or in converted barns. Very often they joined the cast of the play, thus continuing a tradition of amateur theatre which still exists in Henley today.

In January 1777, Lord Villiers of Phyllis Court organised a Gala Week in Henley. A Grand Ball was held on the Wednesday at Fawley Court, the home of Mr and Mrs Sambrooke Freeman (Lord of the Manor of Henley and Remenham). On the Monday and Friday of the Gala Week, plays were staged in a three hundred seat theatre set up in the stables of Mr Anthony Hodges at Bolney Court.

On Monday the play performed was *The Provok'd Husband* by John Vanburgh and Colley Cibber. A verse prologue was written by the Reverend Thomas Powis and was spoken by Lord Villiers, who also played the part of Lord Townly in the play. Other parts were taken by Lord Malden, Mr Onslow (son of Lord Onslow) and Miss Hodges. Mrs Howe and the Rev Powis acted as prompters.

A rehearsal was held on the Saturday before the performance. Mr Hodges' tenants were allowed to attend and also as many of the townspeople of Henley who cared to watch.

The second play was *Pygmalion* by J-J Rousseau. The famous French actor, Tissier, had been engaged to play the leading rôle of the Prince and his statue was played by Miss Hodges. The ladies of Henley were concerned about the employment of a French actor. The awakening of the statue was a delicate part of the play and who could tell how this man from the land of *l'amour* would deal with it.

Caroline Lybbe Powis gives a most graphic account in her diary:

"When the curtain draws up, Tissier is leaning on a table in the most melancholy mood dressed in a most superb habit. At the further end of the stage was a canopy and curtains of gold and silver gauze (which cost £10) behind which was concealed his beautiful statue. He was, I suppose, twenty minutes in all the attitudes of tragic woe deliberating whether he should draw the veil so fearing the sight of this too lovely object. His powers are certainly astonishing. 'Tis said no one equals him. Some partial English flatter themselves their Garrick might come up to him. I own myself of that number, but then, as not a perfect mistress of the French, I fear one's opinion would go for nothing. At last he ventures most gently to draw aside and fasten back the curtain. She speaks. He kneels down, grasps her hand and while they both seem under the most indescribable surprise the curtain drops. It really was the finest scene imaginable and you see avoided every indelicacy."

Caroline Lybbe Powis

The guests at the Ball and also probably at the plays included one Duke, ten Lords, one Count, one General, six Knights, twenty-three Ladies and members of the families of twenty-four prominent local gentry. Mrs Powis notes that, at one of the performances, her son was seated behind Lord Barrymore then aged eight. Later in his life Barrymore was to have a considerable influence upon the circumstances which led to the building of a theatre in Henley.

Billingsgate, Cripplegate, Newgate and Hellgate

Richard Barry was born in Wargrave on 4th August 1769. His mother was Emily Stanhope, daughter of the Earl of Harrington and his father was the Earl of Wargrave. He had an elder sister, Caroline, and later acquired two brothers, Henry and Augustus. When he was just four his father died and, being the eldest son, Richard became Earl of Wargrave, 7th Earl Barrymore, Viscount Buttevant and Baron Barry of Ireland.

Little is known of his early life except that he was tutored by the Reverend John Tickell and his wife, Mary. When Richard was eleven his mother died and he and his siblings were, somewhat casually, looked after by their grandmother, the Countess of Harrington. She died when Richard was fourteen and he was sent to Eton.

Whether it was because of their neglected childhood or some quirk of genetic inheritance, Richard and his three siblings grew up to be wild and eccentric adults. Caroline was nicknamed 'Billingsgate' – a soubriquet which she may have been given by the Prince of Wales because of her loud and frequent use of the kind of language more often heard among fish porters. Henry, who had been born with a club foot, was cruelly called 'Cripplegate' and Augustus was nicknamed 'Newgate' because, it was said, Newgate was the only prison he had never been thrown into. He later became a bishop!

Richard was known as 'Hellgate' supposedly because he had been a member of the Hellfire Club, founded by Sir Francis Dashwood and Francis Duffield, whose family owned Medmenham Abbey. He could not, however, have belonged to the Club since it is generally accepted that it broke up in 1763 after a legal dispute between Dashwood and the Earl of Sandwich on one side and John Wilkes, journalist and Member of Parliament, on the other.

It was, however, an era of 'laddish' behaviour and Richard was a member of several other clubs. He founded the Bothering Club which met at his home in Wargrave. The main object of the club was that

"If any member has two ideas, he shall be obliged to give one to his neighbour".

He was also a member of the Warble Club which held that

"If any member has more sense than another he shall be kicked out of the club".

Despite his apparent self-indulgent lifestyle, he was a sportsman and very fit but his main interest in sport was for the excitement of gambling. He is known to have been an excellent horseman but he lost thousands of pounds on the racecourse. He was a good boxer and is reputed to have won £25,000 on one fight. He was a fine athlete and on one occasion gambled that he could outrun a man on a horse. The contest took place on 16th April 1790. The course consisted of 30 yards to a tree, round the tree and return, the best of four races to decide the winner. The Prince of Wales came to watch and saw Richard manage to win two of the races to claim a draw.

Notwithstanding his youth he became famous – or more likely notorious – around London and earned himself a place in Mayhew's Characters. The cab driver, recalling his father's stories, says,

"One season I used to drive Lord Barrymore in his rounds of the brothels – two or three times a week sometimes."

Another of Richard's interests was the theatre and, in his usual fashion, he pursued it to the extreme. In 1786 he staged a production in a barn of *Miss in her Teens*, a farce written in 1753 by David Garrick. The plot revolves around Miss Biddy Bellair who is in love with Captain Loveit but flirts with Captain Flash and Mr Fribble to spite her aunt who wishes her to marry a rich, older man. The audience consisted of a large number of villagers as well as members of the nobility. Richard played Captain Flash and one diarist wrote that at seventeen, big-boned and six feet tall, he was extremely agile about the stage. So successful was this production that he decided to build his own theatre in the grounds of his house.

'Barrymore', Richard's house, which is little more than a large cottage, still stands at the end of Wargrave High Street, almost opposite Wargrave Hill and close to the St George and Dragon inn. The stables stood opposite the house and Richard had them moved to the other side of Wargrave Hill to the site now occupied by a garage and petrol station. A four hundred seat theatre was built in their place. He engaged Gabriel Cox, the chief carpenter of the Theatre Royal, Covent Garden, as designer and foreman of works and Tobias Young, the scene painter at the Reading Theatre, was called in to assist. There is speculation that an underground passage connected the theatre to the house but, despite considerable searching, no trace of it has been found. The total cost of building the lavishly decorated and ornately furnished theatre was £60,000 (about £4,250,000 in today's terms). It was completed in 1788 and, on 31st January 1789, Caroline Lybbe Powis records in her diary:

"Lord Barrymore had the last year built a very elegant playhouse at Wargrave, had a Mr Young from the Opera House to paint the scenes, which were extremely pretty. His Lordship and friends performed three nights in one week. We were all there on the 31st. It was extremely full of the neighbours and their families. The plays were The Confederacy *and* The Midnight Hour.*"*

She goes on to list the names of the actors and to say that cakes, wine and negus (a beverage made of wine, hot water, lemon juice, sugar and nutmeg named after Colonel Francis Negus who died in 1732) were brought round by liveried servants between the acts.

John Williams, writer and satirist, who wrote under the name Anthony Pasquin, was engaged to be the theatre manager. Later the clown and actor manager, Carlo Dolphini, took over the position. The house next to 'Barrymore' is named 'Dolphins' and this was presumably where Dolphini and any visiting actors were quartered.

In 1790 the theatre was enlarged to seat seven hundred and the stage was lengthened by twenty feet. The Prince of Wales attended the grand re-opening and was so delighted with the evening that he graciously allowed the playhouse to be designated a Theatre Royal. Caroline Lybbe Powis writes in her diary that the plays performed that night were *Figaro* and *Robinson Crusoe*. At the end of the following week Richard celebrated his majority by holding a Masqued Ball in the theatre. Most of Henley's aristocracy attended.

Charles Thomas Carter, the Irish-born musician and playwright, became theatre manager in 1791. Many of his plays and operas were performed including *Blue Beard*, *Just in Time*, *Stand by your Guns* and *Tally Ho!* Those productions and the many others mounted in the theatre attracted much attention in Henley.

At the beginning of 1792 Richard's profligate and expensive lifestyle began to catch up with him. He had lost considerable sums of money to his bookmakers and had borrowed heavily to build and extend the theatre. Gabriel Cox, who had not been paid for his work on the extension, took Richard to court. The sheriff's officers seized the building and made a list of the contents which were later sold. No bid was made for the building and it was eventually dismantled and stored. Much later, between 1850 and 1860, it was purchased by Mr Colleton Garth who had it re-erected as a barn at Castle End Farm in Ruscombe where it still stands.

By the end of 1792 the actors had gone, the captains and the kings departed and Richard had taken a commission in the army. In 1793 his military duties took him to the south coast where his unit was guarding against a possible invasion by Napoleon's army. He was ordered to escort French prisoners from Rye to Dover and at some point along the route he ordered a halt to rest them and his own troops. During the break he took his shotgun to the edge of the beach and had a pot shot at a few seagulls. When he ordered the march to continue he called for his coach to be brought up and as he entered it his shotgun discharged and he was severely wounded in the head. He was rushed to hospital in Dover but was found to be dead on arrival. He was just twenty-four. Richard, as you might expect, did not go quietly to his grave. At the funeral service several of his creditors tried to seize his body and hold it to ransom. He was finally buried in secret in St Mary's Church on 17th March 1793.

In its short life the Theatre Royal in Wargrave had encouraged the growth of an enthusiastic theatre-going community and its closure left a gap in their lives.

The New and Elegant Theatre

Into this theatrical desert John Jonas and Sampson Penley brought their touring company in 1798. They were one of a number of companies who performed the plays of the day and toured around a recognised circuit of small theatres which had been built in the provinces. Jonas and Penley had held the leases of some of these theatres including the Theatre on the Bayle at Folkestone. Theirs was a real family business very much like Mr Crummles' troop in *Nicholas Nickleby*. In addition to Jonas and Penley the troop included Mr W Penley, Mrs W Penley, Mrs S Penley, Miss Penley and Mrs Jonas.

After consultation with William Cox, the tenant of the Broad Gates Inn in the Market Place, they were allowed to perform a season of their plays in the area behind the inn. They commenced their season on Tuesday 18th January with two plays entitled *Everyone has his Fault* and *The Irishman in London*. A playbill for this performance hangs in the foyer of The Kenton Theatre today.

Plays were performed on Mondays, Tuesdays, Thursdays and Saturdays. Caroline Lybbe Powis records in her diary on the 29th January 1798:

"Caroline and I met the Fawley Court Family (the Freemans) at the Henley play; all the gentlemen came to the farce, a very full house and better performers than one could have imagined. The Jew and the Poor Soldier. The company put a hundred pounds into the Henley Bank to answer any demands upon them. Rather unusual for strollers in general."

New Theatre, Henley,
Will open on Tuefday next, January the 16th, 1798,
With a favourite Comedy, called
Every One Has His Fault,

Lord Norland	Mr. NEWMAN
Sir Robert Ramble	Mr. PENLEY
Mr. Solus	Mr. JONAS
Mr. Harmony	Mr. HEALEY
Mr. Placid	Mr. W. PENLEY
Captain Irwin	Mr. GRIFFITH
Hammond	Mr. THOMPSON
Porter	Mr. SHIRELOCK
Edward	Mifs PENLEY
Lady Eleanor Irwin	Mrs. HEALEY
Mrs. Placid	Mrs. PENLEY
Mifs Spinfter	Mrs. JONAS
Mifs Wooburn	Mrs. W. PENLEY

End of the Play, a Favourite Song, by Mr. THOMPSON.

To which will be added, A Comic Entertainment, called,
The Irifhman in London.

Captain Seymour	Mr. THOMPSON
Mr. Calloony	Mr. PENLEY
Murtoch Delany	Mr. GRIFFITH
Edward	Mr. W. PENLEY
Cymon	Mr. JONAS
Louifa	Mrs. PENLEY
Caroline	Mrs. W. PENLEY
Cubba	Mifs PENLEY

Boxes 3s.— Pit 2s.— Gallery 1s.— Tickets to be had at the Poft Office.
Doors to be opened at Half paft Five, and to begin at Half paft Six.
Nights of Performing, Mondays, Tuefdays, Thurfdays, and Saturdays.

Meffrs. JONAS and PENLEY beg Leave moft refpectfully to inform the Nobility, Gentry, &c. of Henley and its Vicinity, that they have neither fpared Pains or Expence in fitting up the Theatre, and that their Company confifts of Performers of diftinguifhed Abilities, and pledge themfelves that their private Character and Conduct will merit their fulleft Approbation, and truft the eftablifhed Reputation with which they have conducted the Firft Theatres of Refpect, will entitle them to a Share of their Patronage during their fhort Stay.

… but not The Kenton Theatre yet!

Mrs Powis' pointed comment about the cash and her praise of the performers would seem to indicate that the Jonas and Penley company was a cut above the average.

The reference to the gentlemen coming to the farce, namely the second play of the evening, is interesting. In the seventeenth century it was the custom to allow members of the working class to see the last two acts of a play free of charge. In the reign of Charles II, however, theatres became less profitable and managers began to charge for late entry. There were complaints from those who felt that they should not pay to see only part of a play and theatre managers began to add a short farce after the main performance to satisfy those customers.

The Penley Company's first visit to Henley seems to have been a resounding success attracting full houses. The population of Henley at the time was between 3,000 and 3,500 and considerable numbers of the nobility and gentry lived in the area. It seemed to be a good business proposition for Jonas and Penley to consider building a permanent theatre.

There was a site in New Street which John Andrew had willed to Robert Kenton in 1503. It was occupied by five cottages which his grandson (also Robert Kenton) had bequeathed to the Corporation of Henley in 1632. They had been used as the town workhouse until 1790 (the year the crew of the *Bounty* mutinied) and now stood derelict. The Corporation was prepared to lease the site and it was acquired by Jonas and Penley to build their theatre. They engaged William Parker, a builder who lived in Henley, to design, plan and erect the new theatre. Mr Mortram of the Theatre Royal, Drury Lane, was engaged to design the décor and supervise the painting. The more hard-headed and practical approach of Jones and Penley resulted in this building costing them just under £2,000. In October 1805, they were able to announce to

"the Nobility, Gentry and others of Henley, and its vicinity, that they have erected, for their accommodation and amusement, a Theatre, equal (if not superior) in convenience and decorations to any of its size in England. The whole of the theatre is designed, planned and executed, under the direction of Mr Parker, builder of Henley. The painting by Mr Mortram of the Theatre Royal, Drury Lane".

The Reading Mercury dated Monday 4th November 1805 contained this advertisement:

"The New and Elegant Theatre, Henley will open on Thursday 7th November 1805 with the very popular Comedy called

*THE SCHOOL OF REFORM
or, HOW TO RULE A HUSBAND
with a farce and other entertainments as will be expressed
in the bills of the day.
Lower Boxes 4s, Upper Boxes 3s, Pit 2s, Gallery 1s.
Doors to be opened at half-past five and to begin at half-past six.
Nights of performing will be Tuesdays, Thursdays and Saturdays.
No person can be admitted behind the scenes.
Tickets to be had at the Post Office and of Mr Penley at Mr Randall's
of whom places for the Boxes may be taken."*

The prices of admission were certainly not cheap in an era when labourers were being paid less than one shilling per day. The same edition of the Reading Mercury contained, on another page, the following headline:

*"FRENCH AND SPANISH FLEETS DEFEATED
DEATH OF LORD NELSON"*

The first production at the New Street building.

Seventeen performances were given that year and the performance on Monday 23rd December 1805 consisted of three plays: *The Point of Honour, The Pulse,* and *The Jew and the Doctor.*

All the takings from that performance were taken to Lloyds Bank on the next day and gifted to the fund which had been set up to help the widows and orphans of those who had been killed at the Battle of Trafalgar.

**Trafalgar was fought a few days before the Kenton opened.
Proceeds from an early production were donated to the widows and orphans of the Battle.**

From Thomas Morton to a pint pot of ale

You will, no doubt, have noted that, although credit was given to the performing company, to the actors, to the man who had designed and built the theatre and even to the man who painted the theatre, no credit at all was given to the author of the play which was performed on that first evening. The *School of Reform* or *How to Rule a Husband* was written by Thomas Morton and first performed at the Theatre Royal, Covent Garden on 15th January 1805.

Thomas Morton was born in the village of Whickham in County Durham sometime around 1764. He was the son of John Morton who died when Thomas was still very young. He was sent to London to live with his uncle, Maddison Morton, a stockbroker, who brought him up as his own son. He attended the Soho Square School where amateur acting was very much in vogue and that, presumably, is where he gained his love of the theatre. One of his closest school-friends, Joseph George Holman, later became a well-known actor.

Morton entered Lincoln's Inn to study law on 2nd July 1784 but there is no record that he was ever called to the bar. His first play, *Columbus*, opened at Covent Garden on 1st December 1792. He wrote thirty plays in all. A further seven plays have been credited to him but they were not successful and he denied having written them. Several of his plays were revived at the end of the 19th Century and, during the same period, he enjoyed a spell of popularity in America. Although his plays are hardly ever produced now, *School of Reform* was presented in November 2005 as part of the bi-centennial celebrations at The Kenton Theatre.

Thomas Morton 1764(?)–1838 who hasn't benefited hugely from repeat fees!

He lived in Pangbourne for many years so it is possible that he visited the New Theatre when one of his plays was being performed. He is described as *"a man of reputable life and regular habits".*

And he was very fond of cricket.

He is one of the select band who became members of the MCC by invitation, most people having to wait for several years before they are elected. He died on 28th March 1838 leaving a widow and three children. Two of his sons were also playwrights. His second son, Maddison, wrote a play called *Box and Cox* which was later re-written by FC Burnand with music by Arthur Sullivan and opened at the Lyceum on 1st November 1847 retitled *Cox and Box*.

After a successful opening, the New Theatre continued to attract considerable business. Mrs Lybbe Powys records in her diary for 12th December 1805 that *"Mrs Atkyns Wright had bespoke a play. We all went to the theatre at half-past six and, despite the weather, Mrs Atkyns Wright had a full house. The plays* The Way to get Married *and* Of Age, Tomorrow".

And on 22nd February 1806 *"At the play* The School for Friends."

Then on 6th March 1806 *"At the play (Mrs Didier's benefit)* To Marry or not to Marry *and the farce* A Tale of Mystery."

Again on 29th March 1806 she went *"To the play to see Cooke perform Sir Pertinax MacSycophant in* The Man of the World *written by the late Charles Macklin and the pantomime of* Harlequin Aesop or Hymen's Gift".

She continued to visit the theatre in 1807 seeing *Adrian and Orilla* on Valentine's Day and *Laugh when you Can* and *The Devil to Pay* bespoke by Lady Stapleton on 17th December. On 22nd December Mrs Lybbe Powys saw *Town and Country* by Thomas Morton and *Blue Beard* both bespoke by Mrs Atkyns Wright with a very full house *"despite the great fog and no moon"* and then on New Year's Eve *"How to Grow Rich* and *Mother Goose* bespoke by Miss Grote of Badgemore."

Mrs Lybbe Powys' diary does not continue very much further. Her husband died soon after and, although she moved to live in New Street (in the large Queen Anne style building opposite Brakspears' brewery), we do not know if she continued to visit the theatre. She died in 1817.

After 1807, the happy state of affairs recorded by Mrs Powys of popular actors, enjoyable plays and full houses began to deteriorate. Jonas and Penley had to take out a mortgage. The attitude towards theatres in general was beginning to change. The introduction of candle-footlights separated the actors from the audience even more than the introduction of the proscenium arch. New plays tackled social situations which the Bible Societies and the Puritan Abolitionists found unacceptable. The upper classes, until then the backbone of theatrical audiences, began to drift away. The rowdy behaviour of some of the playgoers, the quality of the plays being performed and perhaps the quality of the acting, reduced the numbers in the audience and made theatres even less profitable. Perhaps the fact that England was embroiled in wars in Europe and America at this time had an impact on the size of audiences.

The Nobility and Gentry of Henley and its vicinity seem to have followed the general trend and attended fewer and fewer performances. The behaviour of the remaining playgoers deteriorated. On 15th February 1812, William Dicks threw a pint pot of ale into the pit and was arrested for unruly behaviour but the charges were dropped on condition that he made a written apology. His apology was framed and is still displayed in the theatre foyer.

It is worth noting that while William Dicks was penning his apology, Napoleon was setting off on his disastrous march on

---

THEATRE, HENLEY

WHEREAS I WILLIAM DICKS of Newbury, Bargeman, did on Saturday Night laſt, wantonly throw a Quart Mug, with Beer in it, from the Gallery into the Pit of the Theatre, while the Play was performing, which might have materially injured Perſons ſitting therein, for which offence the Manager had me taken into Cuſtody, and commenced a Proſecution againſt me, but on my making this public Acknowledgment of my Offence and paying the Expences already incurred, he has kindly conſented to ſtop all Proceedings; and I hope this will be a Caution to all Perſons not to behave in the like Manner.

(Signed)

WILLIAM DICKS

Henley, February 17, 1812

PRINTED BY G. NORTON, HENLEY

And you *still* can't take drinks into the auditorium.

Moscow; the Luddites were attacking factories in Huddersfield, Halifax, Wakefield and Leeds; Edward Lear, Robert Browning, Elizabeth Barrett and Charles Dickens were born; Walter Scott published his *Lay of the Last Minstrel* and Jane and Ann Taylor were writing *Twinkle, twinkle little star* for their book *Rhymes for the Nursery*.

In 1813 Jonas and Penley, finally unable to sustain further losses, closed the theatre. They sold the lease and moved to Windsor where they took the lease on the newly-erected Theatre Royal.

Limelight, blackboards and pews

Later in 1813 the lease of the New Theatre was taken by

"five trustees acting on behalf of a congregation of non-conformists"

and, for a short time, the theatre was used as a non-conformist chapel. On 9th April 1817, an Act of Parliament establishing National and Industrial Schools came into effect. An unknown benefactor purchased the lease and the building became a National School.

In the same year as the National School was opened, gas lighting was introduced to a number of theatres in England. A few years later, Faraday demonstrated that a piece of lime heated in a hydrogen and oxygen flame gave out a brilliant light. Soon theatrical lamps were being made in which a cylinder of lime was heated in a flame of mixed hydrogen and oxygen. A mirror behind the lime and a lens in front projected a brilliant light onto the stage. Unfortunately these lamps had many practical problems. They operated at a very high temperature and more lime had to be added as it was consumed by the flames. It was also necessary to have a supply of oxygen and hydrogen close to the light and this was usually stored in large gas bags. It took only one small error for a theatre to be totally destroyed. This, in addition to the normal wear and tear on buildings, and the fact that the Kenton was not being used as a theatre at the vital time, is probably an important reason why it is now the fourth oldest theatre in England.

The building was used as a school for many years. Snares Directory records in 1830:

"19, New Street National School Thos Tillet, Master, Srh A. Ollis, Mistress"

and in 1847

"19, New Street. National School John Buckingham, Master, Matilda Buckingham, Mistress."

That was almost the last year that the building was used as a school. In 1848 a subscription was raised to purchase a piece of land for a new school. For the sum of £700 the Trustees of the late Mr George Davenport sold

"a tenement on Gravel Hill and a piece of meadow land, formerly arable or hop, containing two acres, in the parishes of Henley and Rotherfield Greys".

The purpose-built school, which accommodated 520 children of both sexes, was completed the following year at a cost of £2,810-6-9. The pupils and staff moved into the new building and once again the theatre was empty or, as they say in theatrical circles, *"the theatre was dark".*

And it remained dark for almost three years.

In 1850-51 great alterations were planned for St Mary's Church. Work started in 1852. The architect, Benjamin Ferrey, furnished an account of the work for JS Burns' book *A History of Henley*.

"The nave roof, which consisted of a common wagon-headed plaster ceiling, was raised several feet to agree in height with a bay at the east end. A new open-timbered roof throughout was constructed. The ringing floor in the tower was removed and the beautiful groining of the belfry restored and brought to view. A new roof was constructed above the chancel. The east window, previously blocked up by the organ and singer's gallery was restored. The entire chancel was refitted with suitable seating as well as the whole area of the church and a new window inserted at the end of the nave. A new north aisle was built and a new outer wall constructed."

It was impossible to use the church during such dramatic alterations but, fortunately, the theatre was available as a stop-gap. It was consecrated and services were held there until the church was re-opened on Friday 1st December 1854 by the Bishops of Lincoln and Oxford. The church retained the lease of the theatre building and it became the Church Hall of St Mary's Parish Church.

It was used for church purposes for some years until the need for a church hall seemed to recede and it was let out for various other purposes.

About this time references to the building are very confused. It is sometimes called St Mary's Hall, sometimes St Mary's Theatre and sometimes Henley Theatre. It seems to have been given a convenient name depending upon its use, though what it was called when it was used by Brakspears for a spell to store beer barrels, I hate to think. Despite all the changes of occupation, the proscenium arch and the gallery survived.

Christopher Cazenove

Sheila Steafel

For details see small bills

In 1870 there were signs that St Mary's Church Hall was beginning to revert to its original use as a theatre. Kinch's Henley Advertiser of 10th December 1870 reported that a public meeting had taken place in St Mary's Hall in Aid of the Army Scripture Readers and Soldiers Friend Society. On 29th December 1870 the paper reported, in detail, on a Concert given by the Henley Church Choir (Choirmaster Mr Pearson). While both these functions had a religious theme it does seem that the building was being used again for public and entertainment purposes. What happened between 1870 and 1892 is a bit of a mystery but it seems likely that the general use of St Mary's Hall continued.

Early editions of the new local paper, the Henley and South Oxfordshire Standard, reported that the lessee of St Mary's Hall was now GT Savage. This is probably the same GT Savage who owned a shop in Bell Street which sold carpets, linoleum and furniture coverings. Mr Savage arranged a Grand Evening Concert on Saturday 8th October 1892 to celebrate

"The re-opening of St Mary's Hall, for details see small bills".

Five days later on Thursday 13th October (at the New Theatre) the first professional company of entertainers – The Royal Bohee Operatic Minstrels – took the stage with

"Thirty principal Artists – enormous attraction".

Advertisements at this time were, to say the least, picturesque and wildly over-stated usually including the words *"at enormous expense".*

A further 'popular entertainment' of ballads, humorous songs and the like took place on Boxing Day. Doors opened at 7.15 and the show commenced at 7.45. Front seats were priced at 1/-, second seats 6d and back seats (limited) 3d. Tickets in advance were obtainable from Mr Higgins' Library in Hart Street. On the 28th December Miss Heathfield conducted an Evening Concert with mainly local performers. Prices were much inflated. Front seats 3/-, Seconds 2/- and Gallery 1/-.

This, once again, established the tradition of amateur entertainment in Henley.

St Mary's Hall now seems to be firmly established as a place of entertainment once again, but it was not without competition. An advertisement in the Henley and South Oxfordshire Standard on Friday 9th December announced the opening of

"The New Greys Hall, Greys Road. Largest and best ventilated room in the town with Anterooms. To be let for balls, parties, dinners, meetings and entertainments etc. For terms apply to Weyman and Co, South Oxfordshire Furnishing Establishment".

In 1893 another theatre began to advertise in local papers. This was the Royal Gymnasium Theatre which stood in Queen's Street. It seems to have been inoperative for some time but now entered the fray announcing that it would be

"open every week with a change of programme. Singing, dancing and a laughable farce".

St Mary's Hall fought back with no fewer than thirteen productions, professional and amateur, which included plays, operas, minstrel shows, ventriloquists, variety, magic shows and the first showing of the Magic Lantern with a piece entitled *Our Glorious Empire*. Little did Mr Savage know that this form of theatre would become such a popular type of entertainment in the twentieth century.

In 1894 twenty-two groups performed in the theatre. Four of the performances were in aid of various charities and one was mounted to help the Henley Cricket Club of which GT Savage was captain. The Henley Bijou Orchestra made its first appearance in March at a Grand Evening Concert and in April accompanied a gymnastic display by the Henley Volunteers.

On 25th August that year the Royal County Theatre in Reading was struck by lightning and was burned to the ground and much damage was done to adjoining properties. Ignoring all such incendiary risks, the Royal Gymnasium Theatre management announced that they had installed limelight.

For the next two years things continued pretty much as before at St Mary's Hall with a mixture of touring companies, local entertainments, public meetings, rummage sales, cage bird shows and magic lantern shows. On 8th January 1897, the following announcement appeared in the Henley and South Oxfordshire Standard:

"Mr JC Wheeler of the King's Arms Hotel begs to announce that he has taken over the lease of St Mary's Hall from the representatives of the late Mr GT Savage. The Hall will, as heretofore, be available for theatrical and other entertainments, meetings, smoking concerts, dances, dinners, etc. For further particulars and vacant dates apply to Mr Weston, Bell Street Music Warehouse, agent to Mr Wheeler."

That year commenced with a Dramatic Entertainment by the Maidenhead Histrionic Club (President Sir Henry Irving). The Diamond Jubilee of Queen Victoria was celebrated in style in Henley on Tuesday 22nd June. This was recorded by Mr Weston and on 15th November was the subject of a Magic Lantern Show, now referred to as 'Animated Photographs', in St Mary's Hall. The Diamond Jubilee had a much more significant effect on the theatre than was realised at the time. The Town Council decided to celebrate the event by building a new Town Hall and that hall, when it was completed, took considerable business away from the theatre.

Throughout the 1890s more local events were being staged. The Pleasant Sunday Afternoon Society were regular users and various political meetings also took place. There were productions by some touring companies and dances became popular.

An advertisement on 22nd April said that

"A Select Dance will be held at St Mary's Hall on Wednesday 27th April. Dancing from 9 p.m. – 4 a.m. Gentlemen 3/-, Ladies 2/-, Double 4/-".

This is probably the first time that it was accepted that ladies could attend a public dance unaccompanied and they must have been pretty fit if they danced from 9 'til 4!

Gladstone died three weeks later. In October 1898 it could be seen that the old Town Hall was now completely gone. It had been removed brick by brick and rebuilt in another location. Unbelievably, the Town Council were still arguing over the plans for a new one. The foundation stone was finally laid on Friday 9th June 1899 by the Hon WFD Smith MP, who later became First Lord of the Admiralty, and was famously satirised by WS Gilbert in *HMS Pinafore*.

What did Mrs Hamilton do to deserve this?

St Mary's Hall did not celebrate the advent of the Twentieth Century. The fact that a war was raging in South Africa may have dampened the spirits of the local population. In April 'Animated Photographs' of the War were shown. In October 'Living Pictures' were projected using the new Electrograph machine and in November there was a programme by Speer's Grand Cinematograph.

Albert Chevalier, the first real celebrity to appear in the theatre, did so for one night on 2nd July 1900 after a run of four hundred nights at the Queen's Hall in London. He was born in 1861 and was christened Albert Onesime Britannicus Gwathveoyd Louis Chevalier, and made his first appearance on stage in 1869 at the age of eight. He was not from a theatrical family. His father taught French at Kensington School. At the age of fifteen he rejected his mother's desire that he should train for the priesthood and began to write and perform his own songs, soon becoming known as the 'Cockney Laureate'. His best known songs were *My Old Dutch* and *Knocked 'em in the Old Kent Road*. He died in 1923.

Queen Victoria died on 22nd January 1901 but St Mary's Hall was not involved in any mourning. In fact a pantomime, *Babes in the Wood*, performed by Miss Jessie D'Anton and Company opened two days later. The new Town Hall, built to celebrate the Queen's Diamond Jubilee, opened on 13th March two months after her death. Mrs Wood of Shiplake died in the same year at the age of 102 and a photograph of her appeared in the Henley and South Oxfordshire Standard. This was probably the first time that a photograph was printed in this paper. One of the fifteen performances at the theatre that year was an amateur production of two plays in aid of the Henley Cricket Club. The cast included Mr A, Mr F and Mrs A Brakspear, Mr F Crisp and the Misses Janet and Marion Cooper, all members of prominent local families.

The new Town Hall very quickly became the preferred venue for social functions and St Mary's Hall was open on only nine occasions in 1902 despite Mr JC Wheeler's determined advertising campaign. The Gymnasium Theatre had ceased to promote a weekly variety bill and was irregularly used for religious meetings and lectures. Only eight productions took place in 1903 and Mr Wheeler ceased to advertise in August of that year. The Pleasant Sunday Afternoon Society began in that month to use the hall for services every Sunday and only two plays were performed: *The Private Secretary* by CH Hawtry and *Quality Street* by JM Barrie.

No more Pleasant Sunday Afternoons

In 1904, the lease of St Mary's Hall reverted to the Henley Town Council who carried out some repairs and refurbishment and renamed it Kenton Hall. The rent of the hall was set at £40 per annum. The Council minutes for October record that the Town Sergeant, Mr Fox, sought permission to

"engage a boy in the winter months to assist him in his duties which now included the Kenton Hall".

He also applied for an increase in pay. Apart from the continued use by the Pleasant Sunday Afternoon Society on Sundays, Kenton Hall was used on only eleven evenings in 1904. The situation deteriorated even further in 1905 when the Society gave up their Sunday meetings and the hall was used on only seven occasions. 1906 was no better. In that year the hall was used only seven times and these included a Rummage Sale, a Children's Entertainment, a Gymnastic Display and a Benefit Concert. The last event of that year on 12th and 13th December was advertised as 'Jury's Imperial Animated Pictures', the first time the word 'pictures' was used. Other halls were not doing well either. The Royal Gymnasium had given up and was now being used as the YMCA Gymnasium and the Victoria Hall in Grey's Road was doing very little business. The Town Hall, however, with its new and up-to-date facilities, was being used extensively. In the summer months several outside entertainment activities took place in Friar Park and at Phyllis Court.

Something new was added to the list of events at Kenton Hall in 1907. On 30th October Ellis's Cycle Shop held a Clearance Sale during which fifty new and used bicycles were auctioned off. In addition several perambulators and sewing machines were sold and finally a 9HP De Dion Regal Motor Car went to the highest bidder. Unfortunately only six other functions took place that year. In 1909, a new play by a local author received its first performance. This was *Betty's Engagement* by Miss GG Jennings (a descendant of Lybbe Powis' *"beautiful Miss Jennings"* one hundred years before?). It had a cast of local amateur actors who did two performances at 3 pm and 8 pm and, despite a creditable (and lengthy) review in the Henley and South Oxfordshire Standard, it was never seen again.

1910 was an important year in British and Local History. It was a General Election year and in January Mr Valentine Fleming (Conservative) was elected for the South Oxfordshire constituency. Two animated photograph shows were presented at the Kenton Hall in March. King Edward Vll died in May and so, it seems, did Kenton Hall. A number of repairs to the building were carried out in May by Messrs Walden and Cox for a sum of £179. Defective drains caused flooding in the corridor in July costing £10 to repair and, finally, in September the lease was granted to Mr HE Chattel who extended the building at the rear and turned it into a workshop. Once again

"the theatre was dark".

There is no reference to Kenton Hall in any of the Trade Directories from 1911 to 1926. The Town Hall was very busy during this period for all kinds of entertainments and even the YMCA Gymnasium had several shows. The Henley Picture House opened in the old Ice Rink in Bell Street in 1911 showing films and also booking Vaudeville and Variety Shows. Prices were 1/-, 6d and 3d. This form of entertainment at such low prices proved so popular that plans were drawn up for a new purpose-built cinema. Most of the other halls in Henley went out of business leaving the Town Hall as the only live entertainment centre. In 1913 the Church Halls were making themselves available for dances, dinners, parties, meetings and sales and Bronco Bill, who brought his own accommodation with him, set up his circus in Fair Meadow on the Reading Road.

War broke out in 1914 and although there was a good deal of charitable entertainment going on in Henley – at the Town Hall, the Congregational Hall, Trinity Hall and Greys Hall – Kenton Hall remained dark as a theatre. Advertisements in the Henley and South Oxfordshire Standard described the Henley Picture House as

"The largest and most convenient hall in Henley".

The Henley and South Oxfordshire Standard, much reduced in size due to wartime restrictions, at first began to publish a list of local war casualties. In a very short space of time this list took up more than three pages and the paper took to printing only the most recent casualties. Bronco Bill and his circus turned up twice during the war and set up in Fair Meadow to the delight of the local citizens.

After the war it seems that Kenton Hall was being used for the making and storing of theatrical scenery while the Town Hall was in great demand for all sorts of functions including Whist Drives, Recitals, Concerts, Variety Entertainments, Dances, Displays, Baby Shows, Lectures and Jamborees.

On 2nd May 1922 the newly-formed Henley-on-Thames Operatic Society gave their first performance at the Kinema Theatre, Bell Street. The production was *The Mikado* by Gilbert and Sullivan. An enthusiastic critic from the Henley and South Oxfordshire Standard described it as *"the finest amateur performance that has ever been given in Henley"* and hoped that *"this innovation has come to stay"*.

It certainly seemed that it had, for in 1924 Henley-on-Thames Operatic Society gave two more performances in the Kinema Theatre – *When Knights were Bold* and *The Pirates of Penzance*. Later that year the name was changed to the Henley Operatic and Dramatic Society for a production of the play *Are You a Mason?* Several performances were given in 1925; then in 1926 the title was changed yet again to The Henley Royal Operatic and Dramatic Society under the patronage of Princess Mary, Viscountess Lascelles. In February 1929 HRO&DS gave a performance of *The Arcadians* in what was now called the Palace Cinema. In August of the same year the lease of Kenton Hall was due for renewal. At a meeting of the Henley Corporation at the end of July it was stated that Kenton Hall and the adjacent house were governed by the Charity Trustees and a lease of twenty-one years had been granted to the Henley Corporation in 1910 at the rate of £45 per annum. The Corporation then let the Hall and the house at a combined rental of £82 per annum. Mr Watts, Town Clerk, stated that

"the Corporation were really the owners of the property but it was so impregnated with charity that the Charity Trustees had the management thereof and paid over the income to the Corporation".

Mr Watts went on to say that it was a matter of public importance what use the Corporation intended to make of the building. Mr Dee suggested that Kenton Hall should be let for purposes for which the Town Hall was not suitable and Mr Watts agreed. Mr Lloyd said that Kenton Hall had been of great service to the town in years gone by. The Chairman agreed and said that it was a pity that a hall so adequate and so well-equipped should be sealed and kept from the public as it had been during the last twenty-one years. It was finally agreed that

"When approached by the Town Council, the Trustees would be prepared to grant a new lease of Kenton Hall for twenty-one years at £50 per annum with the recommendation that it be used for public purposes".

Thus Kenton Hall in its 124th year and after twenty-one years of closure as a theatre was about to re-open.

Twice nightly – very poor houses

On 28th January 1930, The Rangers Players (2nd Henley Company) performed the first plays at the newly re-opened theatre: *The Tricking of Malvolio* and *The Rational Princess*. Tickets were priced at 5/-, 3/6, 2/- and 1/3 and were available from the Rangers' Company HQ at 33, New Street, just seven doors away from the theatre. Two other performances took place that year – in April a musical *Miss Hook of Holland* by HRAODS (who had recently added the word 'Amateur' to their title) and, in October, *Dawn was Theirs* by the Thames Players who reported

"very poor houses".

The same old confusion existed over the name of the building. The Rangers performed in Kenton Hall, HRAODS at the New Theatre and the Thames Players at the Henley Theatre. Ah, well.

In April, May and June of 1931 three significant events happened in Henley. The first, in April, was the visit to the town of Queen Mary. Several photographs appeared in the Henley and South Oxfordshire Standard and from then on photographs became a regular feature of the paper. Woolworth opened their Bell Street Store on Saturday 16th May at 9 am to great numbers of excited shoppers and on 1st June Mr Cecil Austin took over the lease of Kenton Hall. Cecil Austin was the Managing Director of the Austin Vaudeville Agency and for several months he filled the hall with weekly variety shows starring such popular acts as The Great Ralleano the Boy Wonder (whatever happened to him?) and The Swastika Syncopators (whatever happened to them!). Earlier in the year the Oxfordshire Rural Community Council promoted a Drama Festival – the first of many – in which six local amateur drama groups competed for the adjudicator's favour. Unfortunately, an epidemic of chicken pox swept through Ipsden causing the Ipsden Players to withdraw. The remaining competitors were the Women's Institutes from Greys, Peppard and Benson, the Peppard Village Players and the March Baldon Players. History does not record which team won the Oscar. In October the theatre was closed for redecoration and refurbishment and when it re-opened in November the critic of the local paper was most enthusiastic about the increased comfort for viewing and the improvements which had been made backstage. Cecil Austin had engaged Frank Buckley and his No 1 Repertory Company and they performed four different plays each week until December – a real tour-de-force much praised by the critic. Cecil Austin's tenure ended in December and in that short time he had proved that full-time, efficient management of the theatre could be successful and profitable.

In January 1932 an advertisement in the Henley and South Oxfordshire Standard announced that the theatre was under new management but it seemed to do very little good and only two professional and two amateur productions took place. The situation remained much the same until 1936. There was very little activity until August of that year when it was announced that

"The Management have pleasure in announcing that the Kenton Theatre [sic] will shortly be opening with a first class Concert Party. Popular Prices. Twice Nightly Shows".

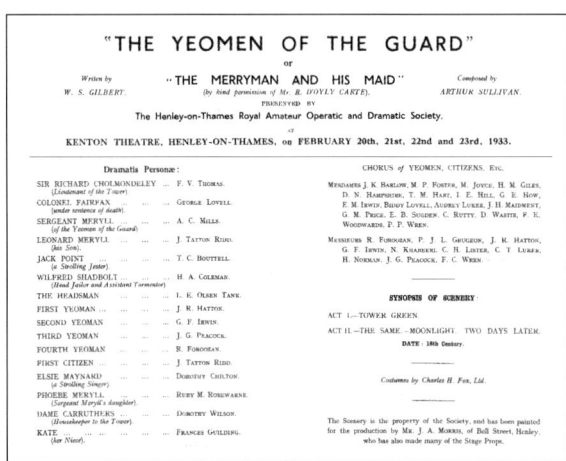

A popular production, typical of the 1930s.

Around that time, thirteen-and-a-half year old Don Hookins left his home at 5, New Street, bypassed the six houses which lay between him and the theatre, and went in to ask for a job. Jimmy Morris, the Stage Manager, was impressed by the youngster's initiative and gave him the job of chocolate boy. He was given a gold and green uniform and sold chocolates at the interval from a large tray – ice cream tubs were not invented until much later. He also had the job of carrying flowers up to the stage for the actresses at the end of a performance and recalls that the same flowers were often used every night for a week.

Charles Wade's Concord Follies opened on Monday 24th August and moved on after three weeks. Their place was taken by the County Repertory Players who, under the direction of Pat Collins and Jack Wood, performed on average two plays each week until the end of January 1937. Two of the plays, *The Volcano* and *Billy's Indiscretion*, were written by Jack Wood and had their first production in December. There is no record that they were ever performed again. Two plays, *While Parents Sleep* and *Sweeney Todd*, were performed by the company at the request of members of their audience. This was a throwback to the early days of the theatre when plays were bespoken (and presumably subsidised) by local theatregoers.

The management of the theatre changed hands at the end of January 1937. The new proprietors were listed as Henley Cinematographic Company and the resident manager was Mr EG Culley. The Zillah Bateman Players were engaged for a repertory season and performed their plays twice nightly (at 6.30 and 8.45). Prices ranged from 6d to 2/6.

The Henley Repertory Players took over from the Zillah Bateman Players in March and performed two plays weekly until the end of May when the theatre closed. It was announced that it would re-open on 2nd August but it was not until 20th September that a new company was found to perform a season of plays. The company was the Thames Valley Playgoers Guild. This group was formed on the initiative of Captain Harold Pullein-Thompson with the assistance of Matthew Forsythe who ran the Forsythe Players at Bexhill. A number of local dignitaries (including the Mayor of Henley and some of the Aldermen) stood as guarantors for the company, obviously eager that Henley should have a permanent theatre. The company performed plays twice nightly until 23rd October when they found that they were unable to continue due to lack of support. Perhaps it was significant that their last play was *It Pays to Advertise*. A production of the Ben Travers farce *Turkey Time* at Christmas was the only other activity of 1937.

Raymond Bennett, brother of comedian Billy Bennett, took over the lease of the theatre for five weeks in March and April 1938 and produced the *Riverside Revels*, a nightly revue, with a change of programme every week. Two other performances had been mounted in January and February, a play, *On the Spot* by Edgar Wallace (which was advertised as being for adults only!) and an amateur variety evening organised by the Henley Townswomen's Guild in aid of Royal

Berkshire Hospital's Extension Fund. A production by Henley Royal Amateur Operatic and Dramatic Society of *Iolanthe* at the end of April was the final production of the year.

A season of plays by the Randall-Newall Players, under the direction of Leo Danvers-Heron, began in January 1939. Despite favourable comments by the critic of the Henley and South Oxfordshire Standard and an offer of 300 free seats for a performance of *Miss Cinders* on Monday 13th February, the group failed to arouse any interest. They were forced to close on 4th March, after a production of *Simple Simon's Baby*, having lost £200 during their season in Henley. The theatre re-opened briefly in April for a one night Variety Concert by Miss Ena Goldsmith and her London Company in aid of Moral Welfare and five performances of *The Arcadians* by the Henley Royal Amateur Operatic and Dramatic Society.

Since the 2nd Henley Company of the Rangers Players opened the theatre in 1930 no one seems to have had any success or made any profit in the management of Kenton Hall. All that, however, was about to change. At the beginning of May the lease of the hall was taken by Sidney Foster. The first thing he did was to change the name to The New Playhouse. The Henley and South Oxfordshire Standard reported:

"The New Playhouse, formerly the Kenton Theatre, New Street, will open again on Whit Saturday, 27th May with new and improved amenities for theatre-goers in every sense of the term. Alterations and redecoration have been carried out, the former including new and up-to-date cloakrooms for both sexes, the provision of additional gangways affording greater facilities for reaching one's seat, modern stage lighting and a bar.

Mr Sidney Foster who has forty years management experience is the mind behind all these costly changes. He has many ideas designed to benefit patrons of the theatre for which 'tons' of new scenery have been purchased. And one of them is the formation of a theatre club."

Sidney Foster also changed the name of his company. Originally called the London Repertory Players, it became the Henley Players and their first production was *Dangerous Corner* by JB Priestley. The play was directed by William Heaven and the proceeds from the first performance were given to the Mayor's Relief Fund. So began one of the most successful periods in the history of Henley's theatre.

A comedy by a local author and dramatist, Sidney Blow, entitled *Lord Richard in the Pantry* was performed for a week in July. Sidney Blow, who lived in Highmoor, personally directed the performances. The play which had been arranged for the week commencing 28th August was *Yellow Sands* by Eden Phillpotts. A film had recently been made of the popular play in which Robert Newton had starred as Joe Varwell. It must have come as a surprise (even to a man of Sidney Foster's experience) when Robert Newton walked into the theatre and offered to repeat on stage the part he had played in the film. Needless to say his offer was accepted and he played to full houses throughout the week. The critic from the local paper said:

"Robert Newton's performance is the finest seen in Henley and should not be missed."

The play closed on Saturday 2nd September 1939. The following morning, Don Hookins, by now Assistant Stage Manager, was dispatched to the station to meet Alec Codrington-Ball who was to appear in the following week's production. Don carried his bags to the theatre and showed him to his dressing room where they listened on Alec's portable radio to Prime Minister Chamberlain declaring war on Germany. The theatre, in common with all other places of entertainment, remained closed during that week. Despite all sorts of restrictions, the theatre re-opened on the following Monday and from then on plays were produced every week.

During the week beginning 27th November 1939 the World Première of Winifred Carter's play *Orchids for Two* took place and a couple of weeks later the theatre closed in preparation for what Sidney Foster dubiously called

"Henley's first pantomime – Dick Whittington and his Cat".

Simon Williams   **Geoffrey Durham**

Support your local theatre

The restrictions of wartime soon began to affect Henley and the theatre. Blackout regulations (the showing of lights after dark was thought to be of advantage to German bombers) meant that considerable work had to be done to prevent spillage of light from the theatre. Meat rationing began in March that year and by October the number of pages in the Henley and South Oxfordshire Standard had been reduced to four. Despite the restrictions Sidney Foster and his Henley Players carried on producing a show every week. William Heaven directed most of the plays (and acted in some) until he was conscripted into the forces in 1941. The younger actors and, later, actresses were also being called up for military service which made it difficult to cast some of the plays. Local amateur or former professional actors were pressed into service.

At first audiences were small as people did not like congregating in large numbers in places of entertainment for fear of bombing. This soon changed, however, as the extra hard work of wartime brought on a need for more relaxation and entertainment and the fear of bombing merely added spice to an evening out. Members of the Forces on leave also sought relief from their duties and most theatres, cinemas and dance halls had half price concessions for those in uniform.

Plays were carefully selected by Sidney Foster and those by respected British (or Irish) authors were the most popular. Emlyn Williams, Somerset Maugham, George Bernard Shaw, Terence Rattigan, JB Priestley, AA Milne and Noel Coward (Britain's favourite author according to Sidney) were the most performed authors at the beginning of 1940. Patrick Hamilton actually came to the theatre himself in February to direct a production of his play *Gaslight*. The Henley Players celebrated the anniversary of their arrival at the Playhouse by holding a dance in the Catherine Wheel. This was advertised as being

"in aid of the Henley Players Fund for New Food and Boots".

The pantomime that year was *Robinson Crusoe* after which the theatre closed for three weeks for alterations and redecoration. The next week the following sad advertisement appeared in the Henley and South Oxfordshire Standard:

"The Playhouse Theatre will be CLOSED NEXT WEEK. As rooms cannot be obtained in Henley for new artists they have had to go home making it impossible to produce next week as advertised Rebecca.

URGENT Wanted at once rooms for artists.

Apply the Playhouse."

As a result of that tearful advertisement the Henley Players were able to continue to produce one play every week and, in fact, managed to perform *Rebecca* two weeks later on 3rd March. This was William Heaven's last play before being called up and his wife, Constance Fecher, played the leading rôle.

In April that year every household received a copy of *If Invasion Comes* and Double Summertime was introduced. In May Sidney Foster celebrated his 100th production by repeating *Dangerous Corner,* the play which had started off his successful tenure as the theatre manager. A celebratory dance was held at the Catherine Wheel on 28th May. Prices were 2/6 in advance or 3/- at the door. Dancing to a military dance band was from 9 pm to 2 am. Advertisements in the Henley and South Oxfordshire Standard contained the phrase

"Dress optional but necessary".

In September, well-known West End actress and film star, Mikki Hood, joined the company and played leading rôles in all the productions until December when her contract ended. The pantomime was *Cinderella*

"with an outstanding cast of 20 performers. Orchestra under the direction of C King-Palmer".

Don Hookins, now aged eighteen, was conscripted into the army early in 1942. He did not return to the theatre after the war but, on his discharge from the Army, he invested his gratuity in starting a small business and was soon to become one of Henley's most respected businessmen.

Mikki Hood rejoined the Henley Players in May 1942 to play Sadie Thompson in Somerset Maugham's play *Rain*. A new War Tax was imposed on theatres that month and prices at the Playhouse had to be raised to 3/6, 3/-, 2/6 and 1/6. Seating in any part of the house could be obtained for 1/6 for the dress rehearsal on Monday nights. The personnel of the Henley Players had almost completely changed in 1942 but Mikki Hood remained as a permanent member. A series of revues was mounted in July and August with Alec Codrington-Ball, Lilian Lee and Mikki Hood as the star attractions. The final revue entitled *Cheerio* included a local talent competition which ran throughout the week. At the final stage of the competition, which took place on Saturday 29th August, the first prize of £5 was won by Sylvia Carr (soprano) of Swiss Farm. The second prize (250 cigarettes) was won by the boy vocalist Peter Harris of 78, Northfield End and the third prize of a 1 lb box of chocolates went to Eileen Gallant (tap dancer) of 15, Greys Hill.

In December the theatre was granted an excise licence which meant that patrons could now enjoy a full bar service. The practice of having the bar open to those not attending a performance was discontinued.

It was becoming more and more difficult to maintain a repertory company in the wartime circumstances and in February after its 172nd production the Henley Players broke up. After a short break Sidney Foster began to engage touring companies to perform at the Playhouse. These included a Russian Ballet company, variety shows and plays. Audience numbers were beginning to fall and it was becoming more difficult to keep the theatre open. Sidney Foster continued his policy of engaging repertory companies for a season and throughout 1944 plays were performed on a weekly basis first by the Chelsea Players then by the Town and Country Theatre. In 1945 the Henley Repertory Company performed until the end of the year with occasional breaks. The Russian Ballet returned but played to very poor houses. In December the Drama Group from RAF Medmenham performed *Squaring the Triangle* by W Gordon Duncalf who also directed. The cast included a young actress, Sarah Churchill, whose father, Winston Churchill, was too busy to attend any of the performances. Her mother, her sister Mary, her brother Randolph and Mr and Mrs Duncan Sandys (her sister and brother-in-law) were in the Wednesday audience accompanied by JG Winant, the American Ambassador. The pantomime had to be cancelled and Foster placed an advertisement in the Henley and South Oxfordshire Standard which read:

"SQUARING THE TRIANGLE."

THE AMERICAN AMBASSADOR AND MRS. WINSTON CHURCHILL AT HENLEY.

"Squaring the Triangle," the R.A.F. Medmenham, Repertory Company's production at the Playhouse this week, is playing to enthusiastic audiences and comes up to the expectations of the majority who have seen it.

The play has nothing unusual about it —just the old story of the nearly-broken marriage with an ultimate happy ending —but it has good and witty dialogue and gives one a keen feeling of enjoyment.

The production is directed by the author, W. Gordon Duncalf, and is slick and well timed. The scenery and lighting effects are good having regard to the limited stage space; the setting of the Mowen apartment is particularly attractive.

Sarah Churchill, daughter of the former Prime Minister, sparkles brilliantly through the play with her attractive voice and personality. She has the gift of making the audience await her every entrance.

Good support comes from William Gordon as Barry Mowen, her affectionate but neglectful husband, while Bob Roberts as Bob Bentley cleverly plays the other corner of the triangle. Pamela Hayes, Enid Phillips and Pauline Growse are extremely attractive in their respective parts. William Franklin as a very efficient manservant, completes the cast.

On Wednesday evening the performance was watched by Mrs. Winston Churchill, the American Ambassador (Mr. J. G. Winant), Miss Mary Churchill, Major Randolph Churchill, and Mr. and Mrs. Duncan Sandys.

The last three performances of the play, the profits of which go to the R.A.F. Benevolent Fund, take place to-night (Friday) and to-morrow afternoon and evening.

On Christmas Eve Mr. Sidney Foster will present the opening performance of his last pantomime in Henley, "Humpty Dumpty," further details regarding which may be seen elsewhere in this issue.

G. C. P.

"It is with great regret that the pantomime has to be cancelled through great difficulties. Firstly, the bad principle of some war-time artists, and secondly, the extra expenses of the present day which, with small seating accommodation one cannot pay. The box office will be open as usual to refund money on advance bookings or money will be returned on receipt of tickets through the post."

This was a strong indication that all was not well at the Playhouse. In February 1946 Sidney Foster, who had been fighting illness for some time, retired and the theatre was closed.

PLAYHOUSE, HENLEY
by arrangement with SIDNEY FOSTER
R.A.F. MEDMENHAM REPERTORY COMPANY
(by kind permission of Group Captain C. H. Cahill, D.F.C., A.F.C.)
presents

SARAH CHURCHILL
in a new Comedy by W. GORDON DUNCALF

Squaring the Triangle
with
PAULINE GROWSE   BOB ROBERTS
WILLIAM GORDON   PAMELA HAYES
ENID PHILLIPS   BILL FRANKLIN

DECEMBER 10th—15th, nightly at 8 p.m.
Matinee Wednesday at 2.30 and Saturday at 5.30 p.m.
In Aid of R.A.F. Benevolent Fund.

Seats Bookable Daily Box Office Opens Dec. 3rd. Seats Bookable Daily
10.30—1 p.m.   2.30—5 p.m.

Commencing Christmas Eve, for Two Weeks, Twice Daily.
SIDNEY FOSTER will present his 194th
PANTOMIME
6th and last in Henley
"RED RIDING HOOD"
Box Office Now Open—Be wise in time: Book Now!

On this occasion the cast was upstaged by the audience!

At the end of May 1946 the Henley and South Oxfordshire Standard announced the re-opening of the Playhouse.

"As many of the public already know, the Playhouse, Henley-on-Thames has been leased by Messrs WH Brakspear and Sons and put under the directorship of Yvonne Le Dain. She is running the theatre under entirely new management and plans to give Henley the best entertainment possible with famous guest artists and try out new plays, keeping a high standard continually. Her work during the war years has been providing theatres in theatreless towns, and she had great success as

the director of the Civic Playhouse, Swindon, as drama manager for People's Plays Ltd, and as the founder of the Rugby Repertory Theatre. Therefore we feel sure that in her capable hands the theatre will become one of which Henley will be justly proud.

New lighting equipment has been installed and the scenery is being renovated and a well-known scenic artist – Miss Elizabeth Dorrity – has been engaged to design the settings.

All this is being done to make this theatre successful; therefore it is up to the Henley public to support it to the uttermost."

The theatre re-opened on Tuesday 28th May, under the auspices of the Henley Theatre Trust, with the play *By Candle Light* by Harry Graham. Jean Forbes-Robertson was guest of honour and appeared the following week in a new play by Winston Clewes and Eugene Leahy, *The Violent Friends*.

The season continued with a different play each week, Yvonne Le Dain often taking one of the parts. She performed her own one woman show at the end of July. In August, presumably in order to encourage playgoers, a system of eight-week season tickets was introduced. The pantomime that year was *Beauty and the Beast* with Rona Anderson as Beauty and Yvonne Le Dain as the Beast. After the pantomime the theatre closed until April 1947.

Despite selecting plays of general interest and, according to local critics, performing them well, the theatre management was unable to attract large enough audiences to make the theatre profitable. Appeals in the papers of the 'support your local theatre' type brought no response and it was decided to call a public meeting in the theatre to discuss the future. The meeting took place on Tuesday 6th May after the first performance of the play *Granite* by Clemence Dane. On the platform were Mr Denham (who acted as Chairman in the absence of Sir Bertram Galer, the Chairman of the Henley Theatre Trust), Mr Chalcraft, Miss Robertson, Dr Staines-Read and Miss Le Dain. The Chairman stated that

"attendances by the general public had not been strong enough to enable the theatre to pay its way and, regretfully, the Director and the Henley Theatre Trust must decide to close temporarily as a considerable loss was being sustained every week".

Yvonne Le Dain outlined several possible ideas for the future including the establishment of a repertory company which would perform for one week in Reading, four days in Maidenhead and two days in Henley. This would help to maintain economic stability, allow for plays to be rehearsed for a fortnight and Henley would be able to keep its own repertory theatre albeit for fewer performances. She hoped to obtain support for this from the Arts Council of Great Britain. Speaker after speaker from the audience insisted that the theatre should not close and a show of hands indicated that this was the majority view. Mr Goyder suggested that those present should buy tickets to give to those people who had never been to the theatre in order to encourage better attendances. By the end of the evening £150 had been contributed to this scheme.

The Henley Town Council held a special meeting on Tuesday 20th May to discuss the future of the Playhouse. Opening the meeting the Mayor (Mr WJ Susman) said that the town owed a great debt of gratitude to the Henley Theatre Trust and to Miss Le Dain for providing such excellent plays which had been much appreciated. The fact remained, however, that the population of Henley and District did not provide audiences sufficiently large to meet the expenses.

The meeting decided to leave the question of continuance or otherwise to the Henley Theatre Trust. Audiences during that week were larger due to the £150 contributed for 'guest' tickets and the theatre remained open until the end of the year. The pantomime, however, was cancelled owing to the illness of Miss Le Dain.

In 1948 only four productions by the Henley Theatre Trust in Association with the Arts Council of Great Britain or the Friends of the Playhouse were mounted in the period up to 6th June. The theatre then closed – again.

On 17th September that year the following advertisement appeared in the Henley and South Oxfordshire Standard:

"The Thames Valley Theatre Trust in Association with the Arts Council of Great Britain are planning to present a season of plays opening at the Playhouse, Henley on Thursday 18th November and at the Pendragon Theatre, Bath Road, Reading on Monday 22nd November with a professional repertory company produced by Basil Coleman late of the Old Vic. Details of times and prices and of the next five plays including a Christmas play for children will be announced shortly. Will you help to establish a permanent professional theatre in Henley and District by becoming a member of

the Trust? Individual donors of £1 are entitled to two seats for the price of one at any of the performances except Friday or Saturday for the first six plays. Six 5/- seats free for a gift of £1.

Donations now, please, to the Thames Valley Theatre Trust at The Grove, Peppard, Henley-on-Thames."

And a few weeks later –

"The Thames Valley All professional Theatre Company in Association with the Arts Council of Great Britain will present George Bernard Shaw's You Never Can Tell at Pinder Hall, Cookham on Tuesday Nov 16, Garrison Theatre, Didcot Wed Nov 17, Playhouse, Henley-on-Thames Thur Nov 18 to Sat Nov 20 and at the Pendragon Theatre, Bath Rd, Reading for the whole week Nov 22 – 27."

Three further plays were produced by Basil Coleman and each was performed at the Playhouse for three days on alternate weeks until the end of the year.

The sequence of performing in Henley on alternate Thursdays, Fridays and Saturdays and in Reading, Maidenhead and Newbury on the other days in a fortnightly cycle continued until the end of April 1949, when, once again, the theatre was closed. An appeal was launched for funds to re-establish the repertory company which had been performing.

A full house greeted the Mayor of Reading when he stood to address a special meeting called on 14th October to discuss the future of the Thames Valley Theatre Trust. The appeal for funds, it was stated, had realised £1002 against a target of £5000. Mr Michael W Summer, secretary of the Trust, explained that the average cost of each production was £530. A fortnight's run of full houses would realise £670 giving a margin of £140. A grant from the Arts Council would cut the cost of each production to £450. He was confident that the venture was a practical proposition. After considerable discussion Captain W Cowley-Miller proposed a vote of confidence in the Trust and asked that the appeal be continued. The motion was passed with five abstentions.

Three companies hired the Playhouse for performances including a show with a full cast of midgets. The 40's decade, one of struggle from beginning to end, finished suitably with *Three Farces for Christmas* by the Mobile Theatre Company.

Richard Todd

Ed Stewart

A small group of local residents

The Thames Valley Theatre Trust had one more show in January 1950, the pantomime *Babes in the Wood*, after which the Tuska Theatre Company took over the lease of the Playhouse. They mounted forty-eight plays during the year, each one being performed for a complete week. There was one gap in their schedule. In February the Henley Royal Amateur Operatic and Dramatic Society recovered from its wartime hibernation and took over the theatre to perform *Robin Hood*, a pantomime by JO Samuel, their first production since *The Arcadians* in 1939. The scenery was designed by John Piper and the piece was directed by the Rev NR Harper Holdcroft. The Tuska Theatre Company had given invaluable assistance during the production and HRAODS expressed their appreciation by giving them a private party at Phyllis Court in March after the performance of *A Murder has been Arranged*. In August Tuska's production of *Born Yesterday* had Diana Dors (described as J Arthur Rank's most glamorous star) playing the leading rôle.

HRAODS continued its revival in 1951 with *Mother Goose*, a pantomime directed by Alec Codrington-Ball who also played the rôle of dame. Alec was a former professional and was well-known in Henley for playing a character called 'Our Sarah' in various revues and variety performances usually accompanied by his partner, Lillian Lee. Seat prices ranged from 2/6 to 5/9. The show was played entirely without a curtain as it had jammed (fortunately in the 'up' position) on the first night.

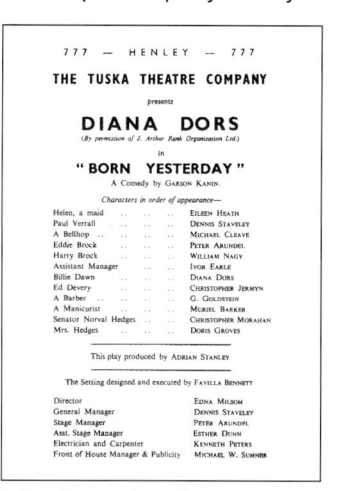

Another major star treads the Kenton boards.

John Piper's proscenium arch of the 1950s.

The theatre was closed until 26th March when the Tuska Theatre Company, directed by Edna Milsom and Charles Cornock, returned for another season of plays. As with other visiting companies they were received enthusiastically at first, then audiences began to drop off and profits began to fall. A meeting of supporters of the company was held in the theatre on Tuesday 15th May to consider the situation and an action committee was formed to raise money to help towards keeping a repertory company at the Playhouse. £75 was raised that night and further sums were promised. It was not enough, however, and the Tuska Theatre Company said goodbye to Henley after a production of *Lovers Leap* on 14th July. Once again the theatre was dark.

This time help was waiting in the wings and on 17th August the Henley and South Oxfordshire Standard announced that Dr AEM Hartley and Mr John Piper had taken over the lease of the theatre. Considerable alterations were carried out both front and back stage. The elegant round-headed windows which had been recently boarded over were opened up and re-curtained. A new raked floor was constructed so that every seat commanded a good view of the stage. John Piper designed a new proscenium arch with Corinthian columns at each side of the stage and a broken pediment above. Two urns in bas-relief with masks of comedy and tragedy as decoration were mounted on the walls on either side. New crimson carpets were purchased and the seats covered in the same colour. The auditorium was redecorated throughout in the late Regency style. The ceiling was dark pink with a gold central medallion and the walls were papered in dark red and dark pink stripes. The orchestra pit was opened up and screened with a dark red velvet curtain suspended on a brass rail. New lighting was installed and new scenery constructed. In celebration of the new look of the theatre it was officially re-named The Kenton Theatre in the middle of August 1951. The local paper enthusiastically declared:

"As the Festival of Britain has drawn to a close, Henley has given birth to a theatre that is going to carry on with the same spirit to show what the people of England can do in the world of art and entertainment."

John Field, a well-known producer who had recently come to live in Henley, was persuaded to take on the production of plays.

"With him there are a number of talented players whose names before long will be household words,"

proclaimed the local critic.

The company included Sara Jameson (Mrs John Field), Adrian Stanley, Beryl Cooke, Joseph Wise, Barbara New, Audrey Sykes, Joseph Shaw, Jane Adams and Peter Nicholls.

The theatre opened on Tuesday 16th October with a production of *The Glass Menagerie* by Tennessee Williams. The Box Office was open from 10 am until noon and from 2 pm until 4 pm and seats (all numbered and reserved) were priced at 6/-, 4/6, 3/6 and 2/6. Performances took place at 7.30 pm on Tuesdays and Wednesdays, 8 pm Thursdays and Fridays and at 5 pm and 8 pm on Saturdays.

On 27th November the World Première of *Regatta Day* opened at the theatre. Written by GO 'Gully' Nickalls (the well-known oarsman) with music by Wendy Williams (wife of the Regatta Secretary), it was described as an Edwardian frolic and qualified for a photograph and a favourable write-up in the Times. Gully Nickalls was himself a member of the cast as was Dr Alan Hartley. John Piper designed the scenery and the show was directed by Peggie Hannen.

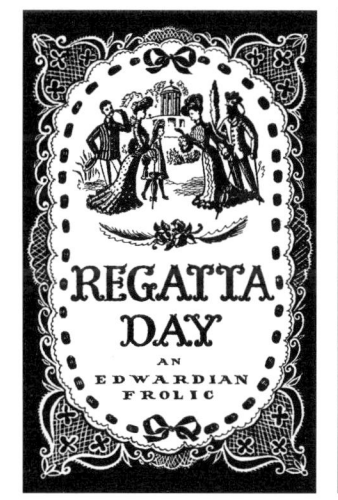

'Gully' Nickalls launches his production in Henley.

Another World Première was presented in 1952. This was *Jinny Morgan* by Howard Spring, the author of *My Son, My Son*. The author attended the first night. In July, John Cranko presented a season of ballet which included Kenneth McMillan and Peter Wright among the performers. The scenery and costumes were designed by John Piper and Osbert Lancaster, the well-known political cartoonist, with Margaret Kaye and Sidney King.

'Let me take you down to Henley . . .'

. . . back in good Victoria's days.
Down the course lies Temple Island
in that distant summer haze. . .

So sang the Leander Boatman in the 1951 and 1952 productions of 'Regatta Day' at the Kenton Theatre, Henley.

In these days when Henley Royal Regatta, the so called 'Last Great Garden Party' has become a haven for big business and company hospitality, 'Let me take you down to Henley' . . . to a much smaller event and a simpler time. A time when the Regatta was as much for the enjoyment of the people of Henley as it was for the visitors, a time when '*Regatta Day*' was playing nightly during the 'steaming' Regatta week of 1952.

'*Regatta Day*' was written by one of the most notable names in Henley's rowing history, 'Gully' G. O. Nickalls. Twice an Olympic silver medallist, he was a member of the winning Grand Challenge Cup crew on no less than seven occasions. He also rowed for Oxford for three years, successfully in 1923 when he was president, and twice won the Silver Goblets and the Stewards Fours. Amongst the cups for international participants in the Regatta is the Nickalls Challenge Cup for Coxless Pairs.

However there was another side to Gully Nickalls, which was surprising for a man so dedicated to the sport of rowing and this was the Gully who had been a soldier, a businessman, an artist and who also passionately loved the theatre, not only as a budding actor but also as a writer. It was from the last of Gully Nickalls' varied interests that the script for '*Regatta Day*' came.

'*Victories and disappointments,*
has this stretch of river known.
Rivalry in deadly earnest,
claiming oarsmen for its own'

Gully may well have had his fair share of victories and disappointments on the water at Henley, but in the Theatre it was victory all the way. Gully Nickalls' involvement with the Kenton Theatre began shortly after its re-opening following the Second World War.

There could probably have been no better subject at the time than that of the Regatta, it was an obvious 'crowd puller' both at its première in the winter of 1951 and even more so during Regatta Week of 1952, when the participants recall how the crowds queued down New Street to get a seat in the Theatre.

The plot was a simple 'boy wants to marry girl' story, the difficulties to overcome were supplied by the girl's over protective aunt and the desire of the leading man to win the Diamonds Trophy.

In true Musical Theatre tradition, our hero, Gerald Thornton (played by the then 17-year-old John Luker) wins the hand of Heather (Mona Sandler, daughter of the violinist Albert Sandler) and the Diamonds, thereby securing a happy ending.

However simplistic the 'boy meets girl' main plot was, it was the subplot that really evoked the spirit of the Edwardian days of the Regatta. There were such cameo roles as the four men (one of whom was Gully Nickalls himself) who were Programme Sellers, Bearded Men, Stewards and who finally portrayed the days when the Nigger Minstrels were a familiar sight on the Regatta Reaches of the Thames.

'*We're programme sellers,*
Just n'ere - Do well fellers.
There's nothing the matter
with Henley Regatta.
It's tame but it increases our earning
And it's not very hard
to get rid of these cards.'

Then there was the Gaiety Girl, Gloria Bellairs played by Peggie Hannen, who is still very much involved in local theatrical circles today. '*Regatta Day*' was also Peggie's directorial debut after ending her time at RADA.

In many ways the characters that Gully Nickalls chose to portray are not so very far away from the characters that we see along the banks of the river during the Regatta today. The Chorus of Debutants were very much like the 'Sloane Rangers' that mill around the Stewards' Enclosure.

Likewise we have only to go down to the boat tents to find a suitable chorus of oarsman. Mitzi, the Viennese opera star played by Helga Mott, a friend of Gully Nickalls brought especially down from London, would today look as though she had arrived a week too early for 'The Henley Festival.' Finally what better occupant for the role of Tim Binder, the Leander Boatman than our own 'boatman' of the Regatta, Tony Hobbs?

'*I've lived by the Thameside since I was a boy,*
a fact I shall never regret.
It's earned my wages and brought me great joy,
and I hope for a few more years yet.
Take a pick of your rivers, the Rhine and the Rhone,

Continued on page four

Peggie Hannen as Gloria Bellairs in the "Leander Dress".

Gully Nickalls (second from the left) with the 'Bearded Men'. Background scenery of Temple Island by John Piper.

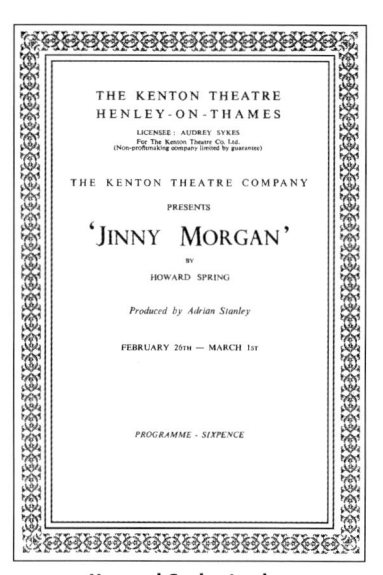

The press make a splash of this production.

THE KENTON THEATRE
HENLEY-ON-THAMES

LICENSEE : AUDREY SYKES
For The Kenton Theatre Co. Ltd.
(Non-profitmaking company limited by guarantee)

THE KENTON THEATRE COMPANY

PRESENTS

'JINNY MORGAN'

BY

HOWARD SPRING

Produced by Adrian Stanley

FEBRUARY 26TH — MARCH 1ST

PROGRAMME - SIXPENCE

Howard Spring's play makes its début.

50

The Henley Players (a local amateur drama group formed in 1948) performed for the first time at The Kenton Theatre in March. Their production of *Love on the Dole* by Walter Greenwood was directed by Edith Devonshire.

It seemed that the name Kenton had, at last, brought success to the theatre but, at the end of 1952, the lease was surrendered and the theatre was closed yet again.

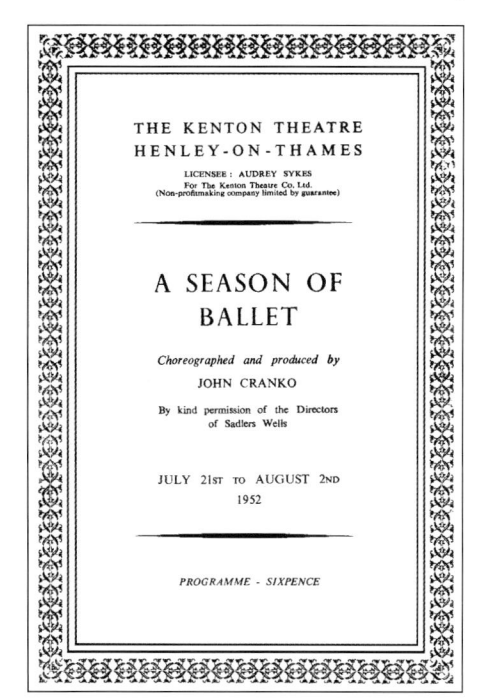

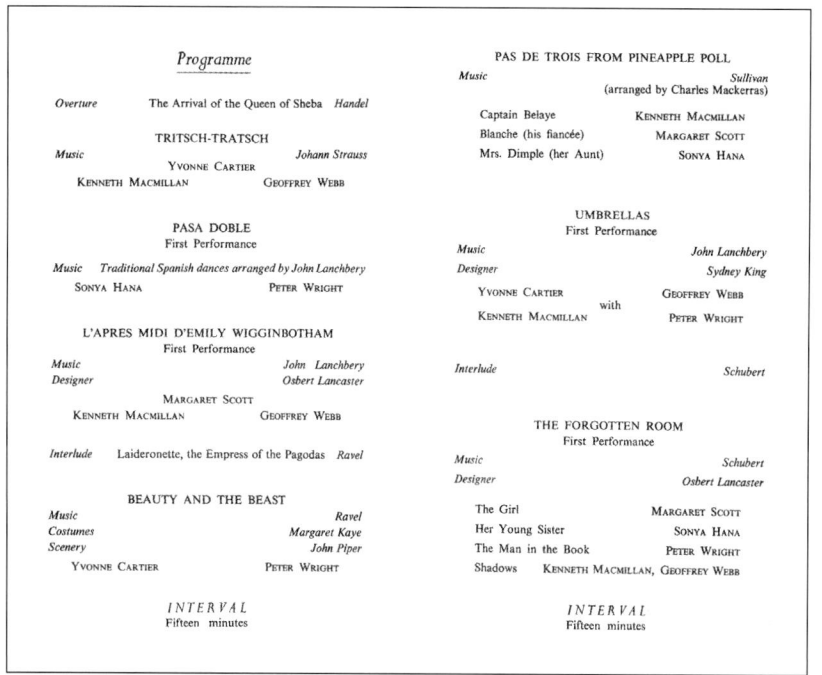

THE KENTON THEATRE
HENLEY-ON-THAMES

LICENSEE : AUDREY SYKES
For The Kenton Theatre Co. Ltd.
(Non-profitmaking company limited by guarantee)

A SEASON OF BALLET

Choreographed and produced by
JOHN CRANKO

By kind permission of the Directors of Sadlers Wells

JULY 21st TO AUGUST 2nd
1952

PROGRAMME - SIXPENCE

Programme

Overture	The Arrival of the Queen of Sheba	*Handel*

TRITSCH-TRATSCH

Music		*Johann Strauss*
	YVONNE CARTIER	
KENNETH MACMILLAN		GEOFFREY WEBB

PASA DOBLE
First Performance

Music	Traditional Spanish dances arranged by John Lanchbery	
SONYA HANA		PETER WRIGHT

L'APRES MIDI D'EMILY WIGGINBOTHAM
First Performance

Music		*John Lanchbery*
Designer		*Osbert Lancaster*
	MARGARET SCOTT	
KENNETH MACMILLAN		GEOFFREY WEBB

Interlude	Laideronette, the Empress of the Pagodas	*Ravel*

BEAUTY AND THE BEAST

Music		*Ravel*
Costumes		*Margaret Kaye*
Scenery		*John Piper*
YVONNE CARTIER		PETER WRIGHT

INTERVAL
Fifteen minutes

PAS DE TROIS FROM PINEAPPLE POLL

Music		*Sullivan*
		(arranged by Charles Mackerras)
Captain Belaye		KENNETH MACMILLAN
Blanche (his fiancée)		MARGARET SCOTT
Mrs. Dimple (her Aunt)		SONYA HANA

UMBRELLAS
First Performance

Music		*John Lanchbery*
Designer		*Sydney King*
YVONNE CARTIER		GEOFFREY WEBB
	with	
KENNETH MACMILLAN		PETER WRIGHT

Interlude		*Schubert*

THE FORGOTTEN ROOM
First Performance

Music		*Schubert*
Designer		*Osbert Lancaster*
The Girl		MARGARET SCOTT
Her Young Sister		SONYA HANA
The Man in the Book		PETER WRIGHT
Shadows	KENNETH MACMILLAN, GEOFFREY WEBB	

INTERVAL
Fifteen minutes

The Kenton attracts leading personalities from the world of ballet.

Three amateur performances took place in 1953 – *Night Must Fall* and *Blithe Spirit* by the Henley Players and *The Gondoliers* by HRAODS. At the beginning of 1954 the Charity Trustees met to discuss the future. It was reported to them that the Henley Players, who had been offered the lease subject to certain clauses including responsibility for internal decorations, had come to the decision that they could not accept some of the clauses and must therefore abandon the idea of taking over the theatre. Alderman Holton spoke of the trouble the Trustees had experienced with the theatre in the past twenty years and felt that, if it could not be let, the only thing to do was to sell it.

After further consideration it was agreed to postpone any decision for one month in order to advertise the theatre to let. In the meantime the building stood empty.

In December the Henley and South Oxfordshire Standard in a contributed article noted:

"The Trustees of the Henley Municipal Charities have granted a lease of the theatre on generous terms to a small group of local residents with the object of preserving this attractive old building for Henley and offering varied entertainment to the district."

Several alterations were carried out by the Trustees to comply with the county fire and safety regulations in order that the premises might, once again, be licensed as a theatre. The new lessees were led by Mr JD Cazes of Shiplake.

The theatre re-opened on 9th December with a stirring fanfare by the Henley Town Band and a spirited prologue written and read by Mr Gully Nickalls. The opening production was *Queen Elizabeth Slept Here* by Talbot Rothwell performed by a group of local amateur actors under the direction of Christine Gwilliam. This was followed by a season of ballet from the Ballets Minerva. It seemed as if the Kenton was again on the way forward.

It had been anticipated that the theatre would open for only twelve weeks of the year and in 1955 that is exactly what it did, staging a good mixture of productions by professional and amateur groups.

In March 1956, the town was shaken by the appearance of the Henley Standard as a compact paper instead of in its previous broadsheet format. That was not all – it had news printed on the front page! The advertisements for The Kenton

Theatre were well placed on the entertainments page and that year the theatre was opened on thirteen occasions. In 1957 the theatre was opened on fifteen occasions. With one exception – the Caryl Jenner Mobile Theatre who had made several visits to the Kenton in past years – all the productions were mounted by amateur companies. Drama festivals were very popular that year. The Oxfordshire Rural Community Council, the National Festival of Community Drama and the Women's Institute all arranged drama festivals. The Henley Standard again surprised everyone by printing their first crossword on 18th January and their first cartoon on 1st March.

All six productions in 1958 were staged by amateur companies. Henley Amateur Operatic and Dramatic Society (the 'Royal' had been dropped a couple of years earlier) had a highly successful production of *Brigadoon* with 'House Full' signs displayed at every performance. John Fowler, a young Glaswegian recently arrived in Henley, was dragooned into playing the bagpipes for this production. John later became Chairman of HAODS and in 1969 was largely responsible for the 'take over' of the management of the theatre by that group. The Henley Standard critic was impressed by the costs of the production of *Brigadoon*. He wrote:

"This is an expensive show and likely to cost nearly £259."

Henley-on-Thames Amateur Operatic & Dramatic Society

presents

"Brigadoon"

A Musical Play

By arrangement with Samuel French Ltd.
Book by Alan Jay Lerner
Music by Frederick Loewe

* * *

KENTON THEATRE

April 15th, 16th, 17th, 18th, 19th, 1958

At 7.30 p.m.

"BRIGADOON"
A MUSICAL PLAY
by
Alan Jay Lerner & Frederick Loewe
PRODUCED BY DORIS PEARCE
CAST:

Tommy Albright	Bill Hedley
Jeff Douglas	John Luker
Donald Ritchie	Dudley Colley
Harry Ritchie	Brian Hewlett
Angus MacMonies	Bill Haffenden
Sandy	Michael Cook
Andrew MacKeith	John Fowler
Fiona MacKeith	Anne Luker
Jean MacKeith	Shirley Hedley
Meg Brockie	Molly Sugden
Charlie Cameron	Toward Davidson-Adcock
Maggie Abernethy	Wendy Tilbury
Mr. Murdoch	Fred Simmonds
Frank	Joe Roop
Jane Ashton	Mary Roop

Ladies of the Chorus
Carole Barraclough, Suzanne Barter, Alice Drury, Joan Fenton, Pauline Finch, Helen Grimshaw, Joyce Hill, Sally Luker, Sherry Pickard, Olwen Saunders, Betty Sugden.

Gentlemen of the Chorus
Raymond Brown, Gordon Bund, John Legh, Reginald Pearce, Gordon Pike, Alan Shepherd.
(Brian Hewlett appears by permission of the Rose Bruford Training College of Speech and Drama).

Bagpipes play in a successful period for the Kenton.

There were twelve openings in 1959. The theatre must have been fairly secure financially for new curtains were purchased at the beginning of the year. The bill (from Rex Howard, King of Tabs) reads:

"1 pair, red velvet tabs   22' x 15'6"
(fully pleated, webbed, eyeleted, taped, fireproofed, weighted)   £37 – 10 – 0
1 border, red velvet   20' x 4'   £10 – 10 – 0
1 border, red velvet   22' x 2'7"   £ 7 – 10 – 0
                                                                                    £55 – 10 – 0"

Those were not expensive times. A bill for a celebratory dance held at Phyllis Court on 13th March amounted to £7 – 16 – 9 and included an item

"Drinks for the Band – 3 shillings".

I don't believe it!!

"This misery which is called a theatre."

The Kenton Theatre Arts Club was formed in 1960. It was a body formed to have discussions and to hear papers on topics connected with the Arts. The Secretary was Mr CRE Gillet of Shiplake. The club met once a month on a Sunday in the theatre. On 9th October Stephen Potter addressed the club on the subject of English and American humour and on 4th December a panel consisting of Professor JA Betts, GO Nickalls, Roger Manvell and Joan Morgan discussed *The Arts in the Age of Television*.

The eight productions in the theatre that year were all by amateur companies. The HAODS production of *Oklahoma!* in April was sold out in advance for all six performances. The Shiplake Players performed a new play by Myfanwy Piper (wife of John Piper) in November.

The number of amateur drama groups in the area had grown and all used The Kenton Theatre for at least some of their productions. A list of groups performing in the 1960's includes

The Associated Counties Theatre Society (ACTS)
Culham College Players
Greys Players
The Henley Amateur Operatic and Dramatic Society (HAODS)
The Henley Players
Henley Drama Club
Henley Catholic Drama Club
Jeanine Greville School
Peppard Drama Group
The Phoenix Players
Shiplake Players
Tamesis Players
Woodley Players

In 1961 and 1962 the operation of the theatre continued as before with local amateur groups mounting all the productions.

Despite appearances things were not going well. On 6th November interested parties were invited to attend a meeting of the Town Council when the future of the theatre was to be discussed. Mr RH Brackston, Chairman of the General Purposes Committee, reported that the Fire Officer had visited the theatre in the spring in advance of a production by a local society. He had filed an adverse report and made recommendations which, if carried out, would mean that the theatre would not be subject to a closure notice. The lessees had assured him that the recommendations would be carried out and that the theatre would not be hired out after the regatta booking to allow the work to be done. Later in the year it came to the Fire Officer's notice that the theatre was to be used again. He made another visit and this time prepared a report which listed thirteen short-term fire precautions. If these were not immediately instituted the theatre would not be allowed to remain open. He also listed twenty-seven long-term recommendations which would have to be complied with if the theatre licence was to be re-issued. The licence was due for renewal at the end of November.

Three local societies, Henley Drama Club, the Henley Players and HAODS, had booked the theatre for their productions at the end of 1962 and the beginning of 1963. Councillor Brackston moved that a licence be issued to allow these productions to take place subject to an undertaking that the thirteen recommendations were carried out. Councillor Weston pointed out that the lessees had already fallen down on their previous promise that the work would be done. He proposed that the work must be completed before the November letting. Councillor Brackston added that his Committee could not recommend to the Town Council that a general licence should be issued until all of the Fire Officer's recommendations had been carried out.

The Council accepted Councillor Brackston's recommendation with the amendment suggested by Councillor Weston.

In 1963 the two remaining productions – *Doctor in the House* by the Henley Players and the HAODS production of *Annie get your Gun* – took place in March and April after which, yet again,

"the theatre was dark".

On the 22nd September that year, Sidney Foster, the man who gave the name 'Playhouse' to the theatre, died at the age of seventy-five. His occupancy was probably the most successful period in the theatre's professional history. After leaving

Henley he had opened a restaurant, The Steak House, at Littlewick Green which proved very popular. Edith Devonshire, who was a member of Sidney Foster's repertory company and who directed many plays for amateur groups, died on the same day.

There is no doubt that in 1963 the building bore very little resemblance to the theatre today. Age had caused considerable dilapidation and the various changes of use and users over the years meant that alterations had been made which were not suited to a theatre. A visitor from Sweden who was shown round wrote to his local paper, The Goteborgs-Posten, describing his impressions.

"The street entrance is big enough to hold ten people. The first thing one discovers as soon as one enters the auditorium is the red-padded seats which look as if they have to prop up each other. One would naturally pull down at least ten or so seats if one tried to sit down. The stage is quite spacious and it is amazing that the floor boards have lasted since the days of Trafalgar. There is also a dress circle and outside this a so-called bar. One carefully climbs the stairs thankful for not falling through the floor straight down into the stalls! The chief inspector of the fire brigade forgot one thing when he ordered the theatre to be closed down, namely the necessity of wearing a crash helmet during visits to the theatre.

The dressing rooms are behind the stage – they had those even in Nelson's time – and also the toilets. No rooms had any privacy at all. This misery which is called a theatre is the pride of Henley and we understand the inhabitants of Henley for being sorry for the closing down of the town's only theatre and thereto one of England's oldest and most well-known theatres."

It seems that, had the Fire Officer not closed the building when he did, it would soon have fallen down. Fortunately, there were a number of people in Henley who were interested in keeping it open. The leaseholders, led by Mr David Cazes, called a public meeting in the Town Hall on 10th March 1964 to discuss the future. The Mayor of Henley, Councillor RH Brackston, was asked to take the chair. Mr Cazes explained to the meeting that, some time before the theatre was closed, he had asked an architect to inspect the building. On his advice Mr Cazes was confident that the building could be made usable again and he suggested an outline programme of mixed professional and amateur productions which he was confident would make the theatre a viable proposition. The architect's proposals would cost about £30,000. He pointed out that another possibility would be to 'patch up' the theatre and return it to its previous condition. This would cost about £6,000 but he pointed out that

"We would still have the same old cold, draughty, poorly-heated theatre with inadequate dressing rooms".

There was an animated and lengthy discussion of these proposals and it was agreed that a committee be formed to examine the minor (£6,000) scheme. The committee was to consist of two members from each of the local amateur dramatic societies, two members of the Henley Society and four or five interested individuals. The Mayor agreed to take the chair. It was to be called The Kenton Theatre Restoration Committee.

Another public meeting was called on 14th January 1965 at which the new Mayor, Councillor Monica Rowe, presided. Councillor Brackston explained that the committee which had been formed had studied the minor scheme and had prepared plans but that they had come up against a 'bombshell' in the summer. It was found that the roof needed repairs which would cost £2,000. In the meantime the lessees had assembled a number of people and had explored the possibilities of the £30,000 scheme. They had failed to get any grants and the costs were such that any profit would soon be wiped out. They had consequently decided not to pursue the matter and had notified the Charity Trustees that they wished to surrender the lease.

The Kenton Theatre Restoration Committee had examined the theatre and had estimated that the essential work required to secure the re-opening would cost approximately £6,000. This was made up of

Electrical work and installations – £750
Fire escape from the bar – £1,000
General fire precautions – £1,200

Roof repairs – £2,000
Repairs to ceiling and a canopy – £1,000

It was suggested that some improvements be carried out at the same time. These would include enlarging the stage by taking in a corridor and the dressing rooms; building new dressing rooms; replacing seats and completely redecorating the theatre. The total, it was estimated, would be in the order of £15,000. It was agreed to mount an appeal for funds to raise this sum.

A new company was formed to take over the theatre lease and on 14th May the inaugural meeting took place. The company was named The Kenton Theatre (Henley-on-Thames) Society Ltd. Mr RH Brackston agreed to become Chairman. Mrs J Moren-Brown was Honorary Secretary and Mr A Punchard, Honorary Treasurer representing his company, Messrs Hallet, Laughlin and Clark. Mr Peter Frankenberg was appointed appeals organiser. The seven founding subscribers were Councillor Monica Rowe (Mayor of Henley), Wing Commander HR Larkin (Chairman of Henley Rural District Council), Lord Rathcreedan (HAODS), Dr T Staines Read (Henley Players), Mr Richard Todd (President of Shiplake Players), Mr Arthur Sharp (Henley Drama Club) and Mrs Daphne Marshall (County Drama Association).

Mr JAR Yeates, the company's honorary legal adviser, told the committee that, following the public meeting, the proposed company had been incorporated on 12th April. An application had been made for it to be registered as a charity. Mr Peter Frankenberg gave details of the fund-raising activities. Henley had been divided into eight districts each with an area organiser and committee. Four hundred people would receive personal calls for help and a further six hundred would be sent literature. He praised Mr David Cazes for the amount of work which he and his committee had done for the theatre in the past and said that this was the last chance of saving the theatre at a reasonable cost. Mr Brackston added that time was not on their side and hundreds of pounds had to be

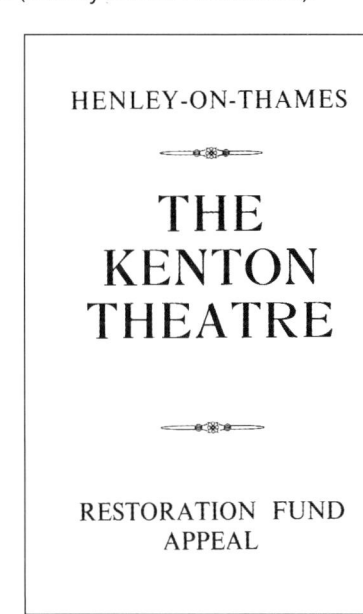

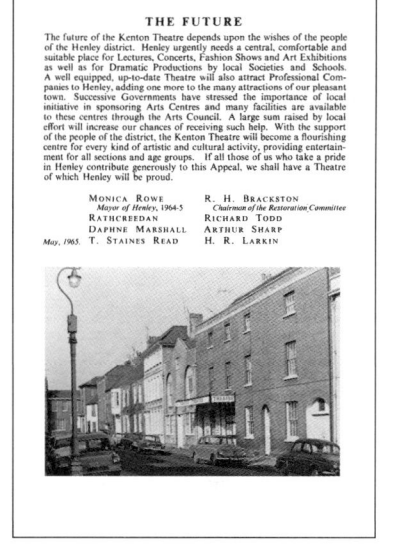

Henley rallies to rescue its theatre.

Celia Johnson supporting the cause.

raised in the next two weeks. He revealed that the first donation had already been received from an elderly lady who liked to attend the HAODS productions. She had handed one pound to the Chairman of that organisation after a recent performance of *The Vagabond King*.

Several of the local amateur dramatic societies began to mount productions in aid of the theatre fund. Margot Thomas directed a production of *Quiet Weekend* by Esther McCracken at Gillot's School and HAODS toured a variety show around the local village halls. Miss Celia Johnson, Lord Rathcreedan and Dr Francis Sheppard addressed a large meeting in the Town Hall on 11th June 1965 when the appeal was officially launched. By the end of June the fund had received almost £4,000. In July the amount totalled £5,396. In August half the money (£7,345) had been raised. In November parts of the theatre were 'sold' for various sums. An anonymous donor 'purchased' the auditorium for £1,000 and HAODS 'bought' the balcony for £500. The help of several national charities was sought. The Chase Foundation contributed £1,000. The Leche Trust donated £500 with the request that it be spent on the entrance foyer. The Oxfordshire County Council made a grant of £500 and the Henley Borough Council £100. The Historic Buildings Council was approached unsuccessfully and the Arts Council later made a grant of £6,500. In addition a seat endowment scheme was in operation and 'buyers' of seats had a name-plaque affixed to the back of their chosen seat. On 12th November the fund stood at £10,448 and by 25th February 1966 no less than £12,489 had been raised.

The auditorium prior to renovation.

Work on the restoration had commenced in October, an offer from Messrs Walden and Son (Henley) Ltd to carry out the building work on very favourable terms having been accepted. Messrs Hammants and Messrs Higgs and Hawkins also carried out work at less than usual rates. Honorary architect, David Tapp, had drawn up detailed plans and reported to the Restoration Committee in December that

"work has been proceeding on retiling the roof which is now two-thirds complete, and replacement of roof timbers is not more than was anticipated. Demolition of the old staircase and surrounding walls has been completed ready for the new staircase to be installed. The demolition uncovered some completely unexpected elements which has meant redesigning the new staircase to overcome some very difficult problems".

Members of the public were allowed, between 6 pm and 8 pm every evening, to inspect the work being done at the theatre in order to show how the appeal money was being spent and to encourage further donations.

At the first Annual General Meeting of The Kenton Theatre (Henley-on-Thames) Society in February 1966 the chairman, Councillor RH Brackston, was able to report that, in addition to work already completed,

"The old stage and dressing room area has been demolished and all the area behind the proscenium has been rebuilt and roofed in. The fly tower will reach roof level within a few days and this will complete all the major structural alterations. Work can then be concentrated on the provision of services, finishes and general redecoration".

Considerable thought had been given to the future operation of the theatre and it was decided that it would be necessary to form a new company to take charge of managing the commercial business of the theatre. It had also been decided that a full-time professional manager should be appointed. Councillor Brackston completed his report by recording his thanks to

"...Mr John Yeates as legal adviser, Mr David Tapp, of Maurice Day and Associates, as architect, Alan Punchard and the firm of Hallet, Laughlin, Clark and Company, our treasurer and Peter Frankenberg our appeal organiser. Their fees for professional services rendered over the past eighteen months, had they been charged, would have run into many hundreds of pounds. In fact, they have all given their services unstintingly and without payment".

David Tapp's designs for the restoration received national acclaim in the Strand Electrical Magazine in 1967. In a series of articles entitled *Design for Drama* the magazine notes:

"*Anyone looking into the theatre now, who saw it before restoration, will be amazed at the work done on a very low budget. It really is going to be a splendid job and the décor chosen by David Tapp, the theatre's brilliant young architect, will set a real seal on the project, which should not only make Henley feel very proud, but*

From the left, John Yeates, David Tapp and Jeremy Langton.

should also give confidence to other ventures in and around the area. Already the first months of the theatre have become heavily booked and enquiries for its use are coming in from many quarters from both professional and non-professional users."

Work continued in the theatre throughout 1966. In October that year Anthony Barlow was appointed Theatre Manager at a salary of £22 per week rising to £25 after a maximum of six months trial period. He took up his duties on 9th January 1967 and set about arranging for the gala re-opening which had been set for 20th March 1967.

The theatre during renovation.

While the work on the auditorium was being done, a new chandelier, the gift of Jeremy Langton, was installed and Albert Parrott removed all the seats to his workshop to be repaired if necessary. With the auditorium free of seats, it was possible to hold a celebratory Ball. Over 300 people in evening dress attended on Friday 24th February 1967. They were treated to dancing from 9.15 pm until 2 am to the music of Barry Fox and his Orchestra and to a cabaret by Pat Chadwick and Lindsay Kemp and his Company. A fork supper was prepared by Mrs Cazes (Chairman of the Ball

The KENTON THEATRE SOCIETY

requests the pleasure of your company at the Theatre for

A BALL

to celebrate the completion of it's restoration

on

FRIDAY, FEBRUARY 24th

from 9.15 p.m. — 2 a.m.

FORK SUPPER

TICKETS £2 - 2 - 0   Dinner Dress
(see over)

… a memorable night.

Committee) and her helpers. Over £400 was raised. It was announced at that time that the money for 100 seats had been donated. Peter Frankenberg appealed for more donations sufficient to make it 200 seats.

The Kenton Theatre re-opened on 20th March 1967 almost four years after it was closed. The first production was *Amphytrion 38* by Jean Giraudoux performed by the Oxford Playhouse Company. The cast included Barbara Jefford, John Turner and Leon Eagles.

Restored and ready for …

It's 'curtain up' again at the Kenton

Evening Post Reporter

LAST NIGHT was a proud occasion for all those Henley people who had faith in the future of the Kenton Theatre. The little playhouse in New Street, which was closed in 1962 as a fire hazard, played to a full house again.

After a five-year struggle in which £20,000 was raised by the people of Henley and spent on a thorough renovation of the Kenton, it reopened last night with the Oxford Playhouse production of Giraudoux's Amphitryon 38.

Tickets for the 300 seats on the first night sold out weeks ago. And on the first night of summer, the lucky holders, many of them people who had contributed to the Kenton's survival as a theatre, crowded into the small foyer well before the curtain rose.

It was a full evening dress occasion, well befitting the dignity of the simply, but tastefully, redecorated auditorium. The fourth oldest theatre building in use in England—one of its first productions was a charity show to benefit the widows and orphans of Trafalgar—soon showed that it had lost none of its theatrical atmosphere.

Until the lights dimmed it was noisy with the laughter and bustle of people who were plainly enjoying themselves.

Before the show the theatre's 24-year-old manager, Anthony Barlow, introduced Lord Rathcreedan, president of the Kenton Theatre Society.

Lord Rathcreedan welcomed prominent visitors, including the Mayor and Mayoress of Henley, Ald. and Mrs. A. R. B. Hobbs, the chairman of Henley RDC, Mr. A. H. Stevens, and Mrs. Stevens, and representatives of the Arts Council, Mr. N. V. Linklater and Mr. Eric White.

Thanking all those who had helped make the reopening possible, Lord Rathcreedan made particular reference to the generous terms which the three main contractors Walden and Sons, Hammants (Henley) Ltd, and Higgs and Hawkins, had given for their work.

He said he hoped that this live theatre would be of special help to young people in Henley and the surrounding district, and that it would include all types of production.

After his speech, with no further delay, the curtain rose on the new Kenton and it was on with the show.

Modern play that is 2,500 years old

AMPHITRYON 38 proved to be an excellent choice for the opening night at Henley's Kenton Theatre. For a celebration like this it was serious enough to keep one's attention, but was still a light-hearted comedy.

The story is 2,500 years old. Jupiter, master of the gods, lusts after Alkmena, faithful wife of the Theban general Amphitryon. He disguises himself as Amphitryon in order to gain access to her bed chamber, and from his successful manouevre, the demi-god Hercules is born.

This play, written in 1929 by Jean Girandoux, is at least the 38th version of the story. Girandoux puts modern vocabulary and ideas into his play. And since most of the players are ancient Greeks and two of them Olympian gods it makes every commonplace 20th century remark seem riotously funny.

We are left quite sure that human nature doesn't change, and, by Jupiter's behaviour, we gather men are made in the image of gods — or does Girandoux really mean that gods are made in the image of men?

The production was very good. John Turner made an excellent laughing Jupiter. Mercury (his son by a previous affair) played by Leon Eagles, makes the perfect foil as a worried little "executive," preoccupied by protocol.

But honours must inevitably go to Barbara Jefford, as Alkmena. With every toss of her head and every drop of her voice she was delightful.

The sets and costumes in last night's production were lighted pinks, blues and yellows — pretty and feminine colours which reflected the dominant note in the play.

MW

■ Amphitryon (Philip Voss) talks with his wife Alkmena, played by Barbara Jefford.

Above: **Amphitryon (Philip Voss) talks with his wife, Alkmena, played by Barbara Jefford.**
Evening Post: Tuesday March 21st 1967.

Top right: **The crowd outside the theatre.**
The Henley Standard: Friday March 24th 1967.

Bottom right: **The Mayor and Mayoress of Henley, Alderman and Mrs ARB Hobbs, pictured with Mr Antony Barlow, the manager, at the opening night performance.**
Reading Mercury: Saturday March 25th 1967.

Kenton opens again

The crowd outside the theatre on Monday evening.

JUST under four years since it last opened its doors for a public performance and 21 months since the £15,000 appeal for its restoration was launched in June 1965, Henley's Kenton Theatre was reopened in fine style on Monday night with the Oxford Playhouse Company's production of the Jean Giraudoux comedy, "Amphitryon 38."

Kenton Theatre re-opens

The Henley Standard, commenting on the building, said:

"The evening was an event to be remembered in Henley and many people expressed favourable reactions on the amenities. The effect of having the bar in the foyer led to a certain amount of congestion however, but this would be alleviated on a less auspicious occasion. The cloakroom facilities are a great improvement, while the fact that more funds are still required was emphasised by the lack of carpet on the floor of the auditorium although the foyer was, in contrast, luxurious. Heating problems have been carefully thought out but people in the front rows experienced

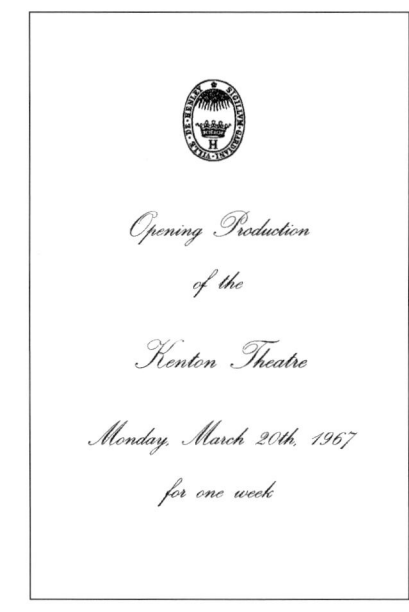

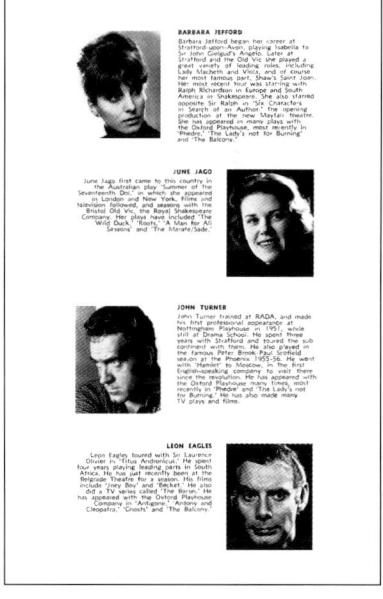

Henley restored as the 'acme of civilisation'.

a slight draught on the raising of the curtains if the doors at the back of the stage happened to be open. The acoustics were good although undoubtedly assisted by the superb voice projection of the actors and actresses".

Not everyone was happy about the re-opening. The following letter appeared in the Henley Standard:

"Dear Sir,

What a deplorable breach of good taste, to put the matter at its lowest level, that Holy Week should have been chosen as the one week in all the year for the long awaited re-opening of the town's famous and ancient Kenton Theatre. Is Henley heathen?

Yours faithfully..."

Stage fright in *The Pyjama Game*?

HAODS were the first non-professional group to perform in the re-opened theatre and their production of *The Pajama Game* opened to great acclaim on Monday 3rd April 1967. The seat prices were

"Monday – Thursday & Saturday matinee – 10/-, 7/6 and 5/-

Friday and Saturday evenings – 12/6, 8/6 and 6/-"

This appears to be the first time that admission prices were dictated by the day of performance as well as the position of the seats.

Now that the theatre was up and running again, it was necessary that the new company which had been agreed at the Annual General Meeting should be formed to operate it. The Memorandum of Association of The Kenton Theatre (Henley-on-Thames) Society allowed it to hold the lease of the theatre and to make all the necessary improvements to allow it to operate but did not permit it to engage in trading. The Kenton Theatre (Henley-on-Thames) Management Society Ltd was incorporated in May and became responsible for the operation of the theatre as a business. The lease, however, continued to be held by The Kenton Theatre (Henley-on-Thames) Society. The Memorandum of Association of the new company states:

"Although given primarily a business function, the management society was, in fact, incorporated as a separate charity, independent of The Kenton Theatre Society. The memorandum of the management society lists its charitable objects which can be taken as a mission statement for the Kenton."

Inevitably the original estimate of £15,000 for the restructuring was exceeded and a further £5,000 was required. The theatre was, however, now open for business and, under the management of Anthony Barlow, bookings were coming thick and fast. A profitable season was anticipated. Of the thirty seven weeks available in 1967, thirty four were booked for a variety of productions. Michael MacLiammoir's one man show *The Importance of Being Oscar* opened on the 15th June. A new repertory company moved into the theatre on 26th June for a five week summer season. Their first play was *The Reluctant Debutante* by William Douglas Home and it was produced by Hubert Woodward in association with Robin Alexander and Cameron Mackintosh. Much later, in 2001, Cameron Mackintosh was to tell Sue Lawley in a *Desert Island Discs* programme that this was his very first production. The cast included Margot Thomas, Simon Williams and Tom Baker. The drama critic of the Henley Standard commented:

Henley-on-Thames Theatre Company Limited
Kenton Theatre
Henley-on-Thames Oxfordshire
Telephone Henley 5698
Theatre Manager A R Barlow

Richard Graham
presents
The Edwards-MacLiammoir
Dublin Gate Theatre
production of
MICHAEL MacLIAMMÓIR
in
The Importance of Being Oscar

June 15th - 17th
Thursday - Saturday at 8 pm
Thurs. Fri. Sat. 12/6 8/6 6/-
Box Office open 10.30 am to 8 pm
Tel Henley 5698

Irish theatre comes to the Kenton.

"The Kenton Theatre's Summer season opens this week with a play which should go down very well. Certainly on Monday evening a large audience received it with enthusiasm. The Reluctant Debutante by William Douglas Home deals frivolously, as the title suggests with the business of the 'deb' season amongst the Mayfair set. It is too frothy to be called satirical – but amusing it certainly is.

After the rather slow first act – during which nothing happens – the play warms up and makes the most of the situations. The acting is excellent – as one would expect from this experienced cast. Paul Bacon speaks with beautiful clarity and plays very smoothly the sophisticated daddy, who, somewhat cynically, pays the vast expenses involved in this marriage market. Margot Thomas matches him very well and makes a convincing socializing mum.

The debutante, reluctant to be led by the nose to some chosen delight, is played by Cheryl Molineaux with suitably youthful enthusiasm – so much so, indeed, that one can hardly accept the plausibility of the romance with the young man whose reputation has so unjustly been slandered. Tom Baker acted this with a quiet integrity which suited the part and contrasted rather well with the callow youth played by Simon Williams. Sarah Buchanan was effective as another mother eager to launch her daughter – well played by Fedore Jones – into society. The play is directed by Michael Gaunt.

Indeed a very successful first night – followed, it is worth pointing out, by a party for the cast and members of The Kenton Theatre Club. This series of carefully chosen plays acted by a professional company deserves to be very well supported."

The same producers mounted a further five plays which, although popular, did not attract the kind of support foreseen by the Henley Standard or the supporters of the appeal fund who had pressed for professional as well as amateur productions. Profits were very small and debts were big and it was decided, after much discussion, to abandon the idea of running the Kenton as a professional theatre. This decision was changed in August when the Management Board was approached by Zack Matalon with a proposal that he would take over the administration of the theatre. Zack Matalon had some experience of theatrical management and he hoped to use the Kenton in conjunction with other theatres where he would be presenting fortnightly seasons of plays. An agreement was signed for an initial period of sixteen weeks commencing on 13th August 1967 and Zack Matalon had the option of extending the period if he wished.

Anthony Barlow, who had been appointed Theatre Manager in October 1966, was unhappy about the change of circumstances in the management of the theatre and tendered his resignation at the Board Meeting on 6th September 1967. He moved to a new post in Watford.

At the same meeting, Alan Punchard, whose company acted as treasurer to The Kenton Theatre (Henley-on-Thames) Society, announced that debts had risen to a total of £6,624. Messrs Hammants, Higgs and Hawkins, Hall and Dixon and Waldens had all agreed to defer settlement of their accounts for two years. At a meeting with one of the creditors, however, Pat Matthews was so unhappy at their uncompromising attitude that he wrote a personal cheque in order to clear the debt. He also arranged for his company, Cassell Arenz and Co. Ltd., to guarantee repayment of a loan of £1,000 from John Lewis and Sons. The operation of the theatre was thus able to continue in the hope that future productions would show sufficient profit to cover the remaining debts.

Zack Matalon's season opened on 10th October with a production of *Anatol* by Arthur Schnizler, and continued to the end of the year with *The Little Hut*, James Joyce's *Exiles*, *The Fantasticks* and *Let Down Your Hair*. The Henley Players marked their return to the Kenton with a production of *Hay Fever* by Noel Coward in November. Attendances at these productions were very small despite Matalon's attempts to encourage theatre goers by offering season tickets, writing to the press and holding public meetings.

The first two productions of 1968 – *To Dorothy, a Son* and *Picnic in Town* – were no more successful. *To Dorothy, a Son* did little to please the Henley Standard critic.

"A chilled and sparse audience may well be forgiven for not having responded with great warmth on the first night of To Dorothy, a Son (Director: Robert Ghisays), Zack Matalon's current production at The Kenton Theatre. In fact, the play is nothing to enthuse about. The plot is probably familiar to most – from film and television if not from the stage – and the verbose dialogue demands more than average acting to make it sparkle."

Matalon declined to take up the option on another season of plays. In addition, he added to the theatre's financial problems by being unable to pay the rental which had been agreed. After a summons had been issued the board decided to accept a mere £200 in full settlement.

At the Annual General Meeting, Bob Brackston, who had been Chairman since the start of the fund-raising campaign, decided to retire from the chairmanship. He felt that the emphasis was now on running the theatre as a business and that someone more qualified than he should take over the reins. John Fowler became the new Chairman.

There were twenty-four productions at the Kenton in 1968, thirteen of which played for one or two nights only. A series of Folk Entertainments arranged by Len Harman introduced well-known artists like Diz Disley and Bob Grant. They were very successful and the Henley Standard described the audience as being

"jam-packed".

A new musical, *Vodka and Tonic*, written by local sisters, Betty Hvistendahl and Annie van Ommeren and performed by the Under 25 Players, had its first performance in August and raised £140 for the Sea Scouts. Local amateur groups supported the theatre with their productions. Unfortunately, one-night lettings were not profitable and the accounts at the end of June recorded an income of a mere £537 and a net deficit of £5,942 despite a grant from the Henley Borough Council. It seemed that the Kenton was about to close once again.

Fortunately, HM Productions, a new company of young, recently qualified drama students had booked the theatre for five nights in December to perform a nightly revue, *Twice Five is Three*, coupled with a children's play, *The King's Prisoner*, performed in the afternoons. The company, managed by David Henderson and Ian Milton, had a successful week and they felt that they could make the theatre pay.

"We're used to working on a shoestring," said David Henderson, "and we understand the difficulties involved in staging a series of plays at the Kenton – but it can be done."

In addition to Henderson and Milton the company consisted of Lucy Henderson, Patrick Connell, Sean McCarthy, Frances Tomelty, Felicity Black (who lived in Henley), Christine Curtis and Tony Rohr.

1969 started off very successfully. After a production of *Rumplstiltskin* by the Grimm Players, HM Productions opened their season with Dylan Thomas' play for voices, *Under Milk Wood*, and continued with a series of well-chosen and well-accepted plays. In March and April various amateur productions by the Henley Amateur Operatic and Dramatic Society, the Henley Players and Henley Grammar School fitted into the schedule and the Finals of the Three-act County Drama Festival took place at the beginning of May.

HM Productions began the second half of their season with the Première of *The Hanging Wood* by Joan Morgan. It seemed that this production would be a guaranteed success. Joan Morgan, well-known local author, playwright and former silent film star, had contributed much to the re-opening of the theatre. The play was based on her book about the notorious local murderess, Mary Blandy, and was sure to attract local interest. Unfortunately this did not prove to be the case. The company found the play difficult and the director, David Henderson, said in his notes:

"My main problems with this play were largely problems of staging. The cast was originally slightly bigger but by some ingenious doubling up arrangements by Miss Morgan we managed to avoid some confusing sub-plot. The language of the time was altogether too high-flown as some of the trial scene illustrates. We have relied quite a lot on lighting and mime in the garden-party and dinner-party scenes. With an inherently dramatic plot, atmosphere is all-important and I have tried to emphasise this with lighting."

The Henley Standard critic was less than kind.

Henley embraces a new breed of playwright.

"I came away feeling as if I had only seen half a play. This was remarkable in view of the fact that the play lasted until eleven o'clock and that the cold theatre made a little discreet dozing impossible. For at times, I must confess, I was very bored. The whole thing seemed to dither unhappily between book and play and Ian Milton, as the Narrator, would have been twice as effective had he been used half as often. The play reminded me of a film trailer."

There is no record of the play being performed elsewhere but, much later, a version modified by Ken Taylor appeared in the *A Question of Guilt* series on BBC television where it was considered successful. Strangely, after the theatre production, stories of a ghost began to circulate…

"I have sensed the spirit of a lady."

It is said that every theatre has its ghost and the Kenton certainly has one but it (sorry, 'she') has been acquired only recently. Before 1969 there were no stories, no rumours, no accounts of strange noises or sudden reductions in temperature, no sightings of strange shapes. After 1969, however, several people, all normal, healthy, unflappable, sober citizens, began to talk of peculiar incidents in the theatre – usually when they were alone.

One lady, working back stage, saw a lady dressed in grey descend the stairs from the dressing rooms as far as the landing then turn left and disappear through the wall. A gentleman, sawing wood on the stage, stopped to rest but the noise of sawing continued for several minutes. Another gentleman alone on stage painting scenery was disturbed by the sound of a plastic cup rolling under the seats. On investigating he could not find the cup. There were several occasions when more than one person observed something odd. A quartet of ladies rehearsing a song on stage clearly saw a lady walk across the back of the stalls under the balcony and walk through the wall into the Green Room passageway. Another group rehearsing a scene from *Hay Fever* was disturbed by a seat in the balcony which, for several minutes, banged up and down. At the same time the temperature on stage dropped noticeably. After a few minutes the banging stopped and the temperature rose.

One common factor in all those sightings was that no-one reported being afraid. It is likely that other sightings or soundings have taken place but have not been reported for fear of embarrassment. In August 2001 the theatre management was contacted by the Ghost Club Society who requested permission to make a study of the theatre.

The Ghost Society was founded in Cambridge in 1851. Founding members included EW Benton (later Archbishop of Canterbury) and Arthur Balfour (later Prime Minister). The London Ghost Club was formed in 1862. Some years later, as a result of a revival of interest in the supernatural, the two bodies merged. In recent years investigations have been carried out in many places including Woburn Abbey, Glamis Castle and the RAF Museum at Cosford.

On Saturday 10th November a group of three members of the Ghost Club Society led by Trevor Kenward, the Administration Officer, accompanied by two members of the theatre management and a lady reporter from BBC Radio Berkshire assembled at the theatre. The study began just before midnight. Control objects were set up in the auditorium and in dressing room number three. Audio tape recorders and video recorders were positioned and operated throughout the period of the study. The emergency lighting remained on. Other than members reporting odd feelings and sensing things, nothing particular happened except that two of the people present were unable to load or operate their cameras, which they would normally have done without difficulty, and there was absolutely no sound from within the theatre itself. Later the audio tape was played back and was found to have recorded strange and unusual noises. Trevor later reported:

"During the time I have spent in this building I have sensed the spirit of a lady, perhaps a person who used to visit this theatre regularly."

Another study took place on 10th April 2004. The same two representatives of the theatre management were present and six members of the Ghost Club Society again led by Trevor Kenward. What took place that night can only be described as startling. Controls, audio and video recorders were all set up as before and the study began about 10.30 pm. Emergency lights were on. At about 11.30 it was decided to try a pendulum session at the back of the auditorium. A number of questions were asked and began to draw responses signified by the movement of the pendulum. By asking appropriate questions, Trevor established that a female spirit was in the theatre and was probably that of Mary Blandy. Questions about the play *The Hanging Wood* brought a considerable response.

An observation session in dressing room three followed after which the group moved once again into the auditorium. This time the emergency lighting was switched off. The theatre was now in total darkness. It was about 1.45 am. Trevor Kenward in his report stated:

"Nothing could have caused the following effect which all the team witnessed. This was a column of light some five feet tall and perhaps a foot wide. Its outline shimmered but it remained fairly consistent in its light frequency being just a white form."

The light moved up and down the aisle then across the seats. It was noticeable that it did not light up the seats as it passed over them. All the people in the auditorium could clearly see and report the position of this light source which moved around the auditorium for about 35 minutes. Trevor took a photograph which clearly illustrated his description.

The emergency lights were switched on again at 2.20 am and, at this time, a pungent smell became apparent and appeared to originate in the orchestra pit. Despite a search of the pit nothing was found which might create such a smell. It dissipated after a few minutes.

The story of Mary Blandy is well known in Henley. She was found guilty of the murder of her father, Francis Blandy the Town Clerk, and hanged in Oxford on 6th April 1752. As a convicted murderer, Mary Blandy should have been buried in unconsecrated ground but instead her body was brought to Henley and buried in the chancel of St Mary's Church between the bodies of her parents. This took place some time after midnight and yet was witnessed by a large crowd of people. Her ghost has been reported in several places including the Little Angel public house, in the grounds of Park Place, in the offices of Blandy and Blandy in Reading and even in the vicarage at Kingston Bagpuize where Mary's cousin was the vicar.

Is this the spirit of a lady?

Barry Howard

John Inman

A place of its own

HM Productions continued their season with *Loot*, *Under Milk Wood*, *Look Back in Anger*, *Waiting for Godot* and *Lysistrata*. None were particularly successful financially and the company was unable to continue. Their last production closed on 1st August. It was *Heartbreak House*.

The Kenton Theatre (Henley-on-Thames) Society was also in financial difficulties. The Honorary Treasurer's report on trading to 30th June 1969 stated:

"The Balance Sheet shows a deficiency, represented by net liabilities, of £15,789. Against this deficiency the estimated gross total of future covenant instalments is £4,000."

No company could continue to trade under these circumstances and it seemed that The Kenton Theatre was about to close again – this time forever.

Pat Matthews, however, came once again to the rescue with a startling proposal. His company, Cassell Arenz and Company would cancel the Society's overdraft, amounting to £7,397, provided that the theatre was, in future, managed on a voluntary basis and it was suggested that the Henley Amateur Operatic and Dramatic Society should take over the running of the theatre. An extraordinary meeting of the society was called for Monday 28th July 1969 at which Lord Rathcreedan took the chair. The Henley Standard reported:

"Mr William Hedley, chairman of HAODS, said that this was the opportunity the Society had long wished for – to have a place of its own. The committee hoped that the body of members would derive real pleasure from being able to use the theatre and considered it a compliment that they should be entrusted with the management. There would, of course, be debts and obligations still standing against The Kenton Theatre companies but proposals would be made for dealing with these financial problems and the day-to-day running of the theatre. These proposals would be subject to the agreement of Pat Matthews, whose company had so generously agreed to cancel the overdraft. The consent of

other creditors, who had very generously agreed that the theatre should be allowed to continue for the benefit of the community, would also be sought.

Mr Hedley then made the formal proposal that HAODS should take over the running of The Kenton Theatre. This was seconded from the floor by Mrs Molly Sinclair and carried by an overwhelming majority."

A formal agreement between The Kenton Theatre (Henley-on-Thames) Society Limited (the leaseholders), The Kenton Theatre (Henley-on-Thames) Management Society Limited (the theatre managers) and the Henley Amateur Operatic and Dramatic Society was signed on 10th November 1969. Under the agreement the Management Society would be the driving force for all activity at the theatre but the reins would be held by HAODS. The main terms of the agreement were:

1. When the agreement came into force, the board and the membership of the Management Society (which had previously consisted of the board of The Kenton Theatre Society) would resign and be replaced by the members of the committee of HAODS.

2. The Kenton Theatre Society would retain its position as the lessee of the theatre but would grant to the Management Society *"the right to occupy and manage the running of The Kenton Theatre on a renewable basis".*

3. The Management Society would pay to The Kenton Theatre Society the net surplus on its management income and expenditure account.

4. Any money gained by fund-raising or grants would be paid to The Kenton Theatre Society and used to repay outstanding debts.

5. HAODS would guarantee that the surplus paid by the Management Society to The Kenton Theatre Society would be at least £500 per annum for two years.

6. The Management Society would observe all the conditions of the Theatre Licence and the Music, Singing and Dancing Licence.

7   HAODS were granted the option (with some conditions) to take over the remainder of the lease of the theatre when all outstanding debts had been repaid.

The agreement made it clear, in its considerations, that:

1   The debt of £5,000 owed to John Lewis and Company would be repaid by The Kenton Theatre Society in six annual instalments of £700 and a final instalment of £800. These payments were guaranteed by Cassell Arenz and Company.

2   The agreement for the lease of the theatre for twenty-one years was deposited with Cassell Arenz as security.

A massive 'clean-up' of the theatre by HAODS members was organised in October by Judy Yeates and after a few more productions the Kenton headed into the 1970's with a clean face, new management and new hope.

Melvyn Hayes   **Moray Watson**

A very successful decade

The new management of the theatre began slowly and there were only thirteen productions in 1970 and twenty-one in 1971, including the World Première of *Annabelle Third Floor* – "a powerful, new, full-scale musical" – performed by the Grimm Players in aid of the RSPCA.

At the Annual General Meeting of The Kenton Theatre (Henley-on-Thames) Society on Wednesday 8th March 1972, held in the Town Hall, Alan Punchard, the Honorary Treasurer, announced to a delighted membership that the theatre was now solvent. A delighted Henley Standard reporter wrote:

"He announced that all local creditors had now been paid and that with cash in hand and money still to come in from covenants there was enough to cover the remaining repayments of the John Lewis Partnership loan. This happy state of affairs had come about by the fact that the theatre's management company (now under the control of the Henley Operatic Society) had contributed just over £3,500 in the past two-and-a-half years towards the reduction of the capital debt.

Mr RH Brackston congratulated the management, saying that it was obvious on visits to the theatre that the fabric is much better cared for and the population at large should recognise the improved atmosphere.

John Fowler, Chairman of the Council of Management, thanked the Henley Corporation for continuing to award a running grant of £300 per annum which had contributed in no small way to the success of the operation."

Bob Brackston took part in another significant event in May of the same year when he presented the awards at the first Kenton Drama Festival. Thirteen amateur companies had taken part and the winners of the Kenton Drama Award were the Wick Theatre Group from Hove. Audrey Laye (a former Secretary of Henley Players) who played the leading rôle shared the Best Acting Award with Simon Kaplin of the Progress Theatre Student Group.

Four well-known writers, Nell Dunn, Peter Porter, EA Whitehead and Shena Mackay, supported by the Southern Arts Association, gave readings and spoke about their work to an interested audience in the theatre on 2nd October. Clearly, the theatre was beginning to move forward with plays and events which attracted an audience.

In December a television film company took over the theatre to shoot the Pantomime Sequence for a film starring Brian Cant and Derek Griffiths. This was the first of many occasions when the theatre has 'appeared' in film or television.

There were twenty productions in 1973 mainly by amateur companies. In June and July Philos Productions had a season of three classic plays which were well received. The theatre closed in August and was completely redecorated. In addition, much to everyone's delight, a new heating system was installed.

The Management and the Executive Committee were becoming more confident and more competent in the management of the theatre. Debts had been paid off and maintenance work, not easy and not inexpensive in a 170 year-old building, was being carried out. Improvements in structure and décor were gradually being installed. With the end of the heavy task of debt repayment, the Executive Committee of the Management Society was able to focus on the management of the theatre. The Executive Committee had been formed in 1969 to include those people who took responsibility for the day-to-day operations. Many of them, including Treasurer Bryan Villars, Front-of-House Manager Nansi Diamond, Bar Managers Rupert Sugden and Gordon Pontin and, on the technical side, Jim Birney and Cliff Colborne, continued in their positions for 10, 20 or even 30 years, to the great benefit of the theatre. The Committee was successfully chaired by John Fowler and Kay Jones in the 70s, Nansi Diamond in the 80s, Cliff Colborne and Christopher Tapp in the 90s and, at the time of the bi-centennial celebrations, by John Reeves.

In March 1978, the Kenton hosted the World Première production of a new play by William Douglas Home. Denys Hawthorne, Marsha Fitzalan, Frank Williams, Ballard Berkley, Julie Breck and Robin Marchel made up the cast of *The Editor Regrets* which was directed by Anthony Roye.

Diana Rigg visited the theatre in April to record a BBC Radio Four programme *With Great Pleasure* before an invited audience.

Diana Rigg.

Sadly, Christina Gwilliam, dubbed 'The Kenton's leading lady' by the Henley Standard, died in October. She had been responsible for much of the work which was done in the sixties to get the theatre back on its feet.

Several new theatre hirers appeared in 1979 – Dave Morgan's Jazz Band, Ballets Minerva and the Maria Rosa Company of Spanish dancers. A new professional company – originally the Henley Theatre Company but later renamed the Henley Repertory Company – was formed by David Tudor to perform at the Kenton. There were thirty bookings in that year and for the first time, Bob Brackston, Chairman, was able to announce to the AGM of The Kenton Theatre (Henley-on-Thames) Society that income from hiring companies had covered expenses and, in addition, that future bookings were excellent. Jennifer Moren-Brown, who had been Secretary since the company was formed, announced her retirement which was regretfully accepted. Mrs Jenny Haywood was appointed Secretary and Joan Morgan and Monica Rowe became Vice-Presidents. A full professional structural survey had indicated that, since the restoration work of the mid-sixties, the building had been kept in good order and that only minor repairs and decoration were required. Plans had been drawn up for the construction of a proper scene dock and paint shop at the rear of the main building.

Obviously the seventies had been a very successful decade and hopes for the future were high.

Sustaining a reputation for World Premières.

Clive Merrison

Lionel Thomson

A far-sighted scheme

The 1980's opened smoothly enough with the theatre being booked on twenty-five occasions and apparently maintaining its successful operation from the previous decade. In 1981, Martin Jarvis, a local builder and Chairman of HAODS, saw an opportunity to make considerable improvements to the foyer. The house, 21 New Street, which was attached to the theatre became vacant. Martin conceived a plan to improve the entrance by incorporating part of the ground floor into the theatre foyer. He also planned to detach part of the garden at the rear to provide an area in which HAODS could build a rehearsal room. This far-sighted scheme did not run smoothly. Planning and listed building consent was obtained but when negotiations were opened between the theatre management and the Charity Trustees concerning the proposal to lease the remaining part of the house as offices and a shop, the Trustees were not enthusiastic. Ernest Leaver, Clerk to the Trustees, explained that, even without an enlarged foyer, there had been a conflict over many years between the residents of 21 New Street and the theatre mainly concerned with noise problems. An appeal was made to the Environment Minister, Michael Heseltine, MP for Henley. He ruled that shops and offices would upset the balance in New Street, which was predominantly residential and increase the parking and traffic problems.

In 1982 an amended plan was put forward. The Charity Trustees agreed to sell the house to Martin Jarvis, subject to the proviso that the

The setting for Henley Players' *Absent Friends*.

upper floors be converted for residential accommodation. The Kenton Theatre Society leased the ground floor for 999 years and plans were drawn up to increase the size of the foyer, to create a bar and a coffee bar and to provide better facilities for the sale of tickets. A longer-term plan to increase the wing area on stage left was also proposed and included an access corridor to the rear of the theatre.

The theatre continued to be busy, averaging twenty to thirty bookings each year. Extra fund-raising events were organised in order to build up sufficient money to give effect to all the plans. In 1985 it was announced that Waitrose were to build a new supermarket in Henley and that this would involve the demolition of the Regal Cinema in Bell Street. There were many loud protests and many local celebrities mounted a show at the Kenton to raise money to prevent the closure of the theatre's rival.

Work started on the enlargement of the foyer in February 1987 after a production of *Salute to Broadway* by the Generation Theatre. The bar, which was situated on the left just inside the door, was ripped out to create space for a new coffee bar and box office. A new modern bar was built on the opposite side of the foyer assisted by a healthy donation from Messrs Brakspear. The kitchen behind the bar was fitted with a dish washer, an ice-making machine and cool storage space and coffee-making equipment was installed at the coffee bar. The building work was carried out by Frank Williams, a local builder. The alterations were planned by Judy Yeates. Inside the auditorium, the lighting desk was moved to a new lighting room constructed at the rear of the circle. This caused the loss of eighteen seats but meant that shows would be better lit.

The foyer was painted in cream and gold, and the entire theatre was covered with carpet which had once graced the floor of the Old White Hart. Decoration work in the auditorium was carried out by volunteers organised by Tom Campbell. The heavy gold stage curtains were bought by Alan and Judith Cluer and the final touch in the foyer was the installation of the elegant chandelier which was provided by an anonymous donor.

The theatre re-opened on 5th March just one month after the reconstruction work had started.

Despite the efforts of the protestors the Regal Cinema closed in February 1989. Plans had been made to construct a new cinema in conjunction with the supermarket. Once again the Kenton management team saw an opportunity and signed an agreement with the former Manager of the Regal, Gordon Mintern, to show films in the theatre. Nansi Diamond, Chairman of the Theatre Management Committee, explained to the Henley Standard that it was not the intention to turn the theatre into a cinema and that live performances would always have priority. She was glad that the theatre could rely on Gordon Mintern's considerable experience and most grateful that he had donated the equipment to the theatre. The first film, *A Fish Called Wanda,* was shown on 20th January 1989, coincidentally on the ninetieth birthday of the artist John Piper who had held the lease of the theatre thirty-eight years previously. Leslie and Marjorie Graham from Marlow were the first to buy tickets and be admitted to the auditorium. Cliff Colborne, who acted as projectionist on that first night and who was to manage the showing of films until the present time, admitted to being more nervous on that occasion than he had ever been in all his theatre experience.

On 30th September in the same year, the rehearsal room, designed by architect Christopher Tapp, was officially opened by actor Robert Hardy who was a Vice-President of HAODS. He named it the Kenton Green Room and wished the Society good fortune for the future. Martin Jarvis welcomed the Mayor, Tony Lane, and Mr David Walden whose company had done the building work. The construction had cost in the region of £120,000 most of which had been obtained as a bank loan, but an anonymous donor had made an interest-free loan in order to get the work started.

Harry Fowler

Roberta Nelson

Entirely due to the people of Henley

The modernisation of the theatre in the late eighties had a good effect on business in 1990. There were thirty-nine bookings that year (including films), audience numbers were high and income increased. In fact, the income increased so much that it attracted the attention of two thieves from Manchester who entered the foyer on 1st May and attacked the box office volunteer who was, at that time, counting cash. They made off with £1,220 despite her attempts to stop them. The police were called and, after a chase, finally arrested the thieves in Culver Lane, Earley.

Further modernisation of the lighting system was installed by Jim Birney in October. With funds raised by his production company, Jim purchased and installed a computerised control system. Jim told the Henley Standard:

"The control desk is portable and has increased the lighting desk capacity from 40 channels to 72 and saves radically the time taken to set up a show's lighting plot."

In the following year, Jim's company, KT Productions, mounted a memorable production of *The Secret Diary of Adrian Mole Aged 13¾* directed by Jan Davy. The cast included sixteen-year-old Kate Winslet as Pandora. The Henley Standard critic, little knowing that he was discussing a future BAFTA and Oscar nominee, noted:

"Kate Winslett [sic] as Pandora improved as the evening progressed. It took her a while to establish herself in the rôle, starting out as a bit of a caricature, but in Act 2 she seemed altogether more comfortable and was, as a result, more convincing."

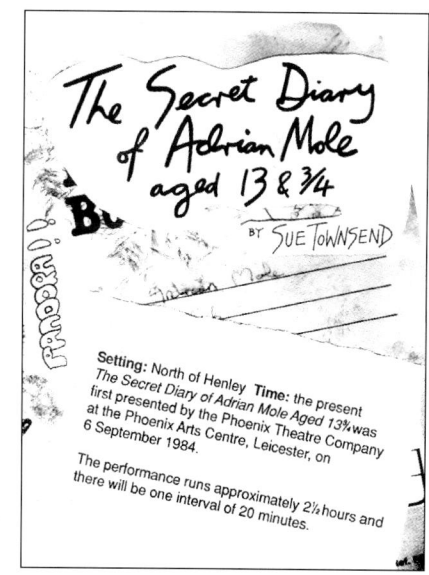

Reproduced by kind permission of Kenton Theatre (Productions).

A storm of protest was raised in 1992 when a bus stop was erected outside the theatre. The residents of New Street were unhappy and the theatre management were concerned that a stationary bus might cause an obstruction if the theatre had to be evacuated in an emergency. The bus stop was later removed. Thirty-eight productions took place in the theatre that year and the Kenton Drama Festival celebrated its twenty-fifth anniversary. John Piper, whose period as lessee in the early 1950s had given the theatre a vigorous start to its modern career, died in July at the age of ninety-five.

The auditorium seating was completely renewed in 1993 as part of the continuing programme of maintenance and modernisation being pursued by the management. In order to raise some of the money for this project, seats were 'sold' as they had been thirty years before and plaques on the backs commemorated those who had donated £100. The theatre, however, was still short of funds and John Legh, Secretary of The Kenton Theatre Management Society, said,

A young Kate Winslet as Pandora.

"We are going to have to be very careful with our money over the next few years."

A record for the number of bookings in one year – a total of 44 – was achieved in 1994. The theatre was obviously enjoying one of the best periods in its long history. One of the men who had been most responsible for this success died in October. John Fowler had been involved in the fund-raising in the early sixties and was the first Chairman of the volunteer management in 1969. John's love of the theatre began when he was asked to play the bagpipes in the HAODS production of *Brigadoon* in 1958.

The author as Bert Baxter.

In the early nineties, the theatre had reported reasonable profits every year. After 1995, however, the opening of the rebuilt Regal Cinema spelt the end of the Kenton's cinema bonanza and the annual results dropped to a mere breakeven position. Nevertheless, throughout the late nineties, bookings continued at a high level and the theatre was able to continue with all the repairs and maintenance required by a two-hundred-year-old building. A generous grant from the Town Council allowed a new heating and ventilating system to be installed which made the building more comfortable for patrons and actors alike. The quality of productions was improved by the purchase of a professional sound system. Plans to extend the wings had been drawn up by Christopher Tapp who was then Chairman of the Management Society, but these had to be held in abeyance until the landlord's consent had been received. This was a nail-biting time as changes in the Charity Laws made it uncertain if permission could be granted. Fortunately permission was obtained and generous grants from both Town and District Councils helped towards the £30,000 required to carry out the work. The result was a considerable improvement in the off-stage conditions and allowed for better staging possibilities.

The lease of the theatre was due for renewal in 2000. If a new agreement was to be reached it would have to be for a longer period than the twenty-one years of the previous lease as many organisations who are prepared to make grants often require twenty-five years of unexpired lease before making them for building projects. For some years the wisdom of having two Societies – The Kenton Theatre (Henley-on-Thames) Society which held the lease of the theatre and The Kenton Theatre (Henley-on-Thames) Management Society which managed the theatre – had been

Here's to the next 45 years

MEMBERS of the Kenton Theatre's governing body raise their glasses . . . to the next 45 years.

They announced that they had completed negotiations with the theatre's landlords, the Henley Municipal Charities Trust, for 45 years — but will have to pay a 'materially increased' rent.

The new lease will enable them to continue the theatre's programme of improvement and modernisation on a secure basis.

Work to extend the wings of the stage was recently completed and further plans for upgrading facilities backstage as well as front of house are under way.

Secretary to the Board Mr Georg Briner said : "We are very happy to have secured the new lease. Unfortunately we have had to concede a material increase in rental charges which we will need to recoup in our operations.

"However, we are confident we can continue to encourage art and entertainment and especially live theatre in all its aspects. Our aim is to make the Kenton Theatre the prime entertainment centre for the area and a place where people of all backgrounds and abilities can take part in creative activities".

The Kenton has occupied its present site in New Street since 1805 and is the fourth oldest theatre in the country still in use as a theatre.

Here's to the future — Kenton Theatre management raising their glasses are (left to right) Pat Port, member of the executive committee, Georg Briner, secretary to the board, Jean Sutherland, member of the executive committee, Bill Port, member of the executive committee and Chris Tapp, past chairman.
R:00.0247.12

The well-trod stage assured for future generations.

under discussion and it was deemed necessary, as a precondition of the renewal of the lease, that the organisational structure of the lessees should be clarified. After considerable discussion under the guidance of Georg Briner, the Secretary of both bodies, the two Societies were merged under the banner of the Management Society thus greatly simplifying the management structure.

Negotiations had begun before the expiry of the lease in 2000 for the Management Society to acquire the freehold of the theatre and a joint valuation of the freehold was undertaken. There were good reasons in favour of a sale.

1   The former Kenton Theatre Society had the preservation of the theatre as one of its main objects.
2   The record of the previous thirty years of major investment and successful running of the theatre as a public amenity.
3   The relatively small income which the Municipal Charities in fact derive from the property.

The landlords, however, broke off negotiations without explanation leaving a new lease as the only option. Negotiations continued on that basis and a lease was granted for forty-five years until 2045.

One of the effects of the restructuring of the theatre management was to end the special status of the HAODS committee members. They had formed the majority of the Management Society Board and membership since 1969. With the membership enlarged by the merger of the two Societies, elections to the new Board would have to be open. John Reeves, who had been Chairman of HAODS, was appointed to the dual position of Chairman of the Board and of the Executive Committee of the new Kenton Theatre (Henley-on-Thames) Management Society. Strong links of joint interest and personal friendship remained between HAODS and The Kenton Theatre.

Kate Lindsey's 2003 costume designs for *A Streetcar Named Desire*.

The theatre celebrated its bi-centenary on 7th November 2005. The fortunes of the building have varied as much as the names which it has been given – The New Theatre, The Congregational Hall, The National School, St Mary's Hall, Kenton Hall, The Playhouse, The New Playhouse and finally The Kenton Theatre.

The thirty-six year period between 1969 and 2005 has been the most successful in its history. This has been entirely due to those people of Henley who have given their time, energy and money to ensure that Henley's Georgian Theatre, the fourth oldest in England, remains an active part of the community.

Kenton Theatre Bi-Centenary 1805-2005

School of Reform
or
How to Rule A Husband

A Comedy in FIVE ACTS BY
MR THOMAS MORTON

Directed by
MR MICHAEL HUNTINGTON

KENTON THEATRE · HENLEY-ON-THAMES

The Kenton Theatre Management Committee invite you to celebrate the 200th Anniversary of the theatre by enjoying the first play ever staged at the Kenton in 1805

Friday 4th - Tuesday 8th November 2005 at 7.45pm

GRAND GALA Monday 7th November at 7.45
Matinee on Saturday 5th November at 2.30 p.m.

ADVANCE BOOKINGS: 0870 770 5899
THEATRE BOX OFFICE: Opens 3rd October 01491 575698

Thomas Morton – setting the stage for another 200 years!

Appendix

List of Seat Dedications at The Kenton Theatre – December 2004

Seats are *Endowed by* unless stated otherwise

ROW A
1. Joan N Mellet
2. The Salisbury Club
3. HK
4. HK
5. AW Stapleton
6. Winifred Hockey
7. Mrs KM Spiers
8. AG Spiers
9. AW Stapleton
10. Mrs Paul Hershon
11. Monica Rowe
12. Lady Rathcreedan
13. Lord Rathcreedan

ROW B
1. WH Smith and Sons Ltd
2. Timothy Whites Chemists
3. Henley Inner Wheel
4. Boots Pure Drug Company
5. Henley Players
6. Dorothy and Arthur Sharp
7. Leslie Langton and Sons Ltd
8. The Henley Society
9. Judy and John Yeates
10. Henley Chamber of Trade
11. The Red Lion Hotel
12. The Red Lion Hotel
13. Agatha Christie

ROW C
1. The Wargrave Gymkhana
2. Henley Branch National Council of Women
3. Henley-on-Thames Round Table
4. General Decorating Supplies Ltd
5. Phyllis Yablon
6. GS
7. The Leander Club
8. Dr BJ Pirquet
9. Henley Townswomen's Guild
10. Henley Townswomen's Guild
11. Shiplake Players
12. Shiplake Players
13. The Horlick Charitable Trust

ROW D
1. Phyl-Mayo Gift Shop
2. Phyl-Mayo Gift Shop
3. Hill-Mayo Antiques
4. Hill-Mayo Antiques
5. Pat Matthews
6. Audrey Matthews
7. Sally Hardy
8. Robert Hardy
9. Maude Crougey
10. *In memory of* Gwyll
11. Christine Gwilliam
12. Henley Drama Group
13. Henley Drama Group

ROW E
1. Grace and Scott Underwood
2. Ross Henley and Lorna Trow
3. Miss DM Ive
4. *In memory of* Claudia Emily Culbard
5. Cynthia Wrigley Dunkerley
6. Associated Counties Theatre Society
7. Leah Corlett
8. Eric Batemen
9. Mary Clifford and Jasmine Weaver
10. Mrs Falcon and Mr and Mrs JHL Scott
11. William Duncan
12. Joy and David Stewart
13. Stuart Turner Ltd

ROW F

1. Aubrey Watson Ltd
2. Mrs GL Rosemond
3. Mrs M Marcham
4. The Kenton Theatre Club
5. Henley Football Club
6. Mr and Mrs HFC Dalston
7. The Administrative Staff College
8. John and Myfanwy Piper
9. The Honourable W Fraser
10. Mrs AH Whipham
11. DV
12. Ann Woolf
13. John Woolf

ROW G

1. Joy Good
2. Sid Glass
3. Charles Luker
4. The Honourable Mrs SM Whitamore
5. Percy Reeves
6. The Oxfordshire Technical College
7. Waitrose Ltd
8. Greys Youth Fellowship
9. WH Brakspear & Sons
10. Sydney Green & Sons
11. St Mary's Youth Club
12. Lady Brunner
13. Sir Felix Brunner

ROW H

1. *In appreciation of* **Freda Fairbairn** *from the Kenton Theatre Management 1992*
2. Denis Pearce
3. Pat Curran
4. Jack
5. *In memory of* **Wing Commander John Moffett**
6. Flavia Pickworth
7. Mrs Constance Toomey
8. Doris Isaac
9. Molly Sinclair
10. Lewis Cowan
11. Diane Todd
12. Sarah McAlpine
13. Alistair McAlpine

ROW I

1. Garth Diamond
2. Nansi Diamond
3. *In memory of* **Audrey Dolly Stoner**
4. Mike Hurst
5. Heelas (Reading) Ltd
6. Rainer Pannier
7. *In memory of* **Hilda Bessie Weyman**
8. *In memory of* **Flavia Pickworth**
9. Judith Cluer
10. Andy and Wendy Allum
11. *In memory of* **Albert Parrott**
12. Friends of Jill Hole
13. The Burgermeister of Leichlingen Karl Ruel *1978*

ROW J

1. Richard Todd
2. *In memory of* **Jack Carson-Bury** *1915 – 1991*
3. Associated Counties Theatre Society
4. Wendy and Georg Briner
5. Grey's WI
6. Rainer Pannier
7. Mr H Harly-Burton
8. Mrs Molly Harly-Burton
9. Alan and Evelyn Shave
10. Henley Players
11. Colin and Jean Lynes
12. Mena Marshall
13. *In memory of* **Bernard Marshall**

ROW K

1. *In appreciation of* **John Leigh** *Theatre Secretary 1969 – 1994*
2. Isobel Carson-Bury
3. Peter Cubison
4. Janice Cubison
5. Peter and Betty Nunn
6. Pip and Phil Hughes
7. Robert Wyane Hughes
8. Lucy Jarvis
9. Dean Beedell
10. Monica and Martin *Horse & Groom*
11. *In memory of* **Molly and Rupert Sugden**
12. Hilda Dobson
13. *In memory of* **Gertrude and Elsie Loton**

ROW L

1. Jennifer and Barrie Scott
2. Graham Cross
3. Muffin Hurst
   Henley Children's Theatre School
4. *In the memory of*
   Malcolm H Dickinson
5. *Endowed for*
   "My Girl" Sally Jayne Buttle *August 2000*
6. *In memory of* **Gabby Derbyshire** *1994*
7. Kenton Theatre (Productions)
8. *Dedicated to the memory of* **Jean Este**

ROW M

4. HAODS
5. HAODS
6. HAODS
7. HAODS
8. HAODS

ROW N

1. Pat and Bill Port
2. *In memory of* **Irene Tapp**
3. Jackie and Tony Hobbs
4. Wendy and Keith Graham *WLOS*
5. *In memory of* **Gwyn Lloyd** *WLOS*
6. *In memory of* **Harry Scarrott** *WLOS*
7. Keith Baker *WLOS*
8. *In memory of* **Doris Goatley** *WLOS*

ROW O

1. *In memory of*
   Pat Port *Henley Players – August 2000*
4. Michael Huntington and Julie Davis
5. Geoff Bamford *Lighting Designer*
6. John Wyatt *WLOS*
   In memory of a good friend who died suddenly 1999
7. Marilyn Baker *WLOS*
8. David Rust *WLOS – 50 years on stage – 1998*

ROW Q

1. Elizabeth Moon
2. Sandra Moon
3. Wendy Sargent
4. Nick
8. *In memory of* **Doris Clive-Spencer**
   Chairman Kenton Theatre Festival 1972 – 1996
9. *In memory of* **John L Clive-Spencer**
12. *In memory of* **Anthony Hannen**
13. Lutena Meller and Eric Yates
14. Gordon and Jo Pontin
15. Richard J Durkin *HAODS 1991 – 1993*

Productions at the Kenton Theatre

1805	**The New Theatre**	
Nov 7	School of Reform or How to Rule a Husband	Jonas & Penley Co ,,
Nov 12	The Soldier's Daughter and The Wags of Windsor	,,
Nov 14	Douglas and Love Laughs at Locksmiths	,,
Nov 16	Who Wants a Guinea and The Spoil'd Child	,,
Nov 26	Pizarro or The Death of Rolla and The Devil to Pay	,,
Nov 28	The Honey Moon and Love Laughs at Locksmiths	,,
Nov 30	Who Wants a Guinea and Raising the Wind	,,
Dec 3	The Gamester and Don Juan	,,
Dec 4	Lover's Vows and Two Strings to your Bow	,,
Dec 7	The Rivals and The Turnpike Gate	,,
Dec 12	The Heir at Law and My Grandmother	,,
Dec 14	The Way to get Married and Of Age Tomorrow	,,
Dec 16	The Poor Gentleman and The Hammer of the Alps	,,
Dec 17	The Honey Moon and Don Juan or The Libertine Destroyed	,,
Dec 19	Pizarro or The Death of Rolla and The Irishman in London	,,
Dec 21	The Soldier's Daughter and Wags of Windsor	Jonas & Penley Co
Dec 23	The Point of Honour and The Pulse and The Jew and the Doctor	,,
1806		
Feb 22	The School for Friends	Jonas & Penley Co
Mar 6	To Marry or not to Marry and A Tale of Mystery	,,
Mar 29	The Way of the World and Harlequin Aesop or Hymen's Gift	,,
1807		
Feb 14	Adrian and Orilla and Forty Thieves	Jonas & Penley Co
Dec 17	Laugh When You Can and Devil to Pay	,,
Dec 22	Town and Country and Bluebeard	,,
Dec 31	How to Grow Rich and Mother Goose	,,
1870	**St Mary's Hall**	
Dec 8	Public Meeting	
Dec 29	Henley Church Choir Concert	
1892	**St Mary's Hall**	
Oct 8	A Grand Evening Concert	
Oct 13	The Royal Bohee Operatic Minstrels	

Dec 26	*A Popular Entertainment*	
Dec 28	*Evening Concert*	Miss Heathfield

1893 St Mary's Hall

Jan 1	*Mike*	Mr Alfred Robertson's London Co
Jan 19	*Our Boys*	,,
Jan 20	*Johnny*	John Nash
Feb 6	*Maritana* and *Rose of Auvergne*	Mr Calder O'Beirne and his London Opera Co
Feb 7	*Faust*	,,
Feb 8	*Balfe* and *The Waterman*	,,
Feb 13-15	*Christiana* and *Hulme Minstrels*	JB Howard
Apr 27	Grand Meeting and Entertainment	The Primrose League
May 15	*Saved*	Victor Raynar and his Criterion Concert Co
May 16	*Naval Engagement* and *Magic Mirror or The Artists Dream* followed by a laughable farce	,,
Jun 17	Special appearance of Lieut Walter Cole the Great Ventriloquist and his Merry Folks	
Sep 22-23	Grand Miscellaneous Entertainment and *Jack's Wife*	Mr Milton Welling's Vaudeville Company
Oct 30/Nov 1	*Billy the Buccaneer*	Bert Artlett & Will Rayner's Celebrated Burlesque Pantomime Company
Nov 6-7	*The Midnight Bell* Great Dramatic & Scenic Productions	Hybert & Liddle
Nov 29-30	*Ups and Downs of Life*	Miss Marguerite Merryweather Company
Dec 1-2	*The World's Mystery*	Duprez, Monarch of Magicians
Dec 12-13	*The Solicitor*	Mr Herbert-Basing's London Company

1894 St Mary's Hall

Jan 15-16	My Sweetheart	Miss Isabel Mart's No 1
Jan 23	*A Grand Entertainment* Amateur Theatricals *Yellow Roses* *A Fair Encounter* *Incompatibility of Temper*	The Primrose League Henley Habitation 638
Jan 29-30	*Ruth's Romance* and *The Old Master* and *Pitcher and Tosser*	Mr Charles Hartley & his London Dramatic Company
Feb 21-22	*Red Riding Hood* and *Little Bo Peep*	
Mar 7	A Grand Evening Concert	Members of the Henley Bijou Orchestra
Mar 26-27	*Aladdin or An Old Lamp in a New Light*	GT Savage presents Mr John W White & Co
Mar 29	*Living Pictures* with Music POSTPONED	
Apr 2-3	Gymnastic Display *An Assault at Arms* plus a farce *Chiselling* and Selections by the Henley Bijou Orchestra	Henley Volunteers
Apr 5	*The Solicitor*	Mr Herbert-Basing's Company

Apr 6	*Rip Van Winkle*	,,
Apr 12	Entertainment	Maidenhead Amateur Minstrels
Apr 13	Living Pictures with Music	GT Savage
Apr 18	Public Meeting	Conservative Party
Jun 4-5	*Tom's Mother-in-Law* preceded by *A Peculiar Fix*	Mr Clement Forrester-Jones and Co
Jun 14	An Entertainment	GT Savage
Aug 23-25	*Merry Dick Whittington*	Miss Jessie D'Alton's Company
Sep 10-1	London Society Entertainment	Mr Frederic de Lara's Company
Oct 1-6	Mon – *Faust* Tue – *East Lynne* Wed – *My Sweetheart* Thu – *Christmas Carol* Fri – *La Fille de Madame Angot* Sat – *Corsican Brothers* Each evening will conclude with a variety concert and a laughable farce.	Mr Victor Rosini's Spectral Opera & Drama Company
Oct 22-23	Grand London Combination	Mr J Olenzo's Co Of Star Artistes and Performers
Oct 29-30	*Silver King*	Mr Wilson Barrett's Co
Nov 14	Banjo Concert	The Pierrot Banjo Team
Nov 21-22	*Uncle Tom's Cabin*	Mr JA Hybert's Co
Nov 27	A Variety Entertainment	Ladies and Gentlemen of the neighbourhood

1895 St Mary's Hall

Jan 21-22	*Our Eldorado*	La Comedie Anglaise Co
	Miss Madge Merryweather	
May 15	A Grand Miscellaneous Conce	Holy Trinity Church
Oct 14-16	*The Little Widow* preceded by *Meeting Place*	Mr Leonard Robson & London Co

1896 St Mary's Hall

Jan 8-9	The Henley Poultry, Pigeon, Rabbit, Cat, Cavie and Cage Bird Show	EH Fox & WJ Tranter
Jan 30/Feb 1	*On the Briny*	Charles Williams Co
Feb 17	*Trilby*	
Mar 17	The Band of the 2nd Volunteer Batallion Oxfordshire Light Infantry and A humorous sketch entitled *How the Cat* and concluded with a laughable farce entitled *Virginian Mummy*	
Apr 6	Grand Entertainment with a laughable sketch called *Oh! What a Day*	The Henley Drum & Fife Band
Apr 21-22	A Grand Gymnastic Display of the Church Institute plus a laughable farce entitled *The Steepchase*	The Gymnastic Class Athletic Club
Apr 23	*A Bunch of Violets*	Mr Beerbohm Tree's No 1 Company
May 4	Royal Bohee Operatic Minstrels	JD Bohee Company
May 6	A Great Rummage Sale	
May 28-30	*Secret of a Life*	Mr Sidney Bowkett Co
Aug 6-7	*A Woman of No Importance*	Mr HW Varna Co
Sep 30	*The New Barmaid*	Mr Austin Fryer's Co
Oct 20	Moore and Burgess Minstrels	
Nov 11	*The New Barmaid*	Mr HW Varna Co
Nov 16-18	*Men of War*	Mr Nelson Watts-Phillips Co

Dec 1	Professor Du Cann Premier Ventriloquist of the World plus a Farcical and Rural sketch entitled *Turnip – Top Village* and a laughable farce in three acts entitled *The Egyptian Mummy*.	Mr Neville Lynn Co
Dec 7-8	*The Lady Slavery*	Mr A Barry Storr and Company
Dec 14	A Grand Entertainment and *Bammy* a screaming farce	
Dec 15	A Concert	The Misses Del Riego
Dec 26-29	*The Housebreaker* preceded by *Matrimonial Squabbles* and *Lady Audley's Secret* preceded by *Tomesbust*	JJ Delmage & London Company
Dec 30	A Concert	The Misses Del Riego

1897 St Mary's Hall

Jan 6	A Dramatic Entertainment Triple Bill: *Bad Penny*, *Sunset* and *The Matrimonial Agency*	Maidenhead Histrionic Club (President Sir Henry Irving)
Jan 13-14	Grand Exhibition of Poultry, Pigeons, Rabbits, Cats, Cavies and Cage Birds	CT Passmore & EH Fox
Jan 18	A Concert	The Misses Del Riego
Jan 21	*The Sign of the Cross*	Ben Greet Company
Feb 2	Grand Variety Entertainment	Reading Banjo & Mandolin Band
Feb 3	Grand Meeting and Entertainment	Primrose League Henley Habitation
Feb 10	A Concert	The Misses Del Riego
Feb 16	*Dick Whittington* and *The Man in the Moon*	Lewis and Dysart Company
Feb 26	A Grand Entertainment	
Mar 2	A Concert	The Misses Del Riego
Mar 8-9	*A Harvest of Wild Oats* and *East Lynne*	Hubert Bartlett Company
Apr 5-6	*An Irish Girl and her Sweetheart Pat*	Harry Monkhouse Company
Apr 9	A Grand Entertainment and a laughable sketch *Leave it to me*	Henley Drum & Fife Band
Apr 28	Evening Concert	Mrs Ada Watson
May 3	Gymnastic Display	Church Institute Athletic Club
May 5	Rummage Sale	Henley-on-Thames Parochial Fund
May 10-12	*My Artful Valet*	C St John Denton
May 24-26	*Pet of the Empire*	Miss Pattie Verona's Burlesque Company
Oct 25-26		Mr Charles Graham's No 1 Vaudeville Company
Nov 8-9	*The Wages of Sin*	
Nov 15	Queen's Diamond Jubilee Procession Animated Photos and Lieut Walter Cole and his Merry Folks And Refined Comic Concert and Operetta Company	
Nov 22-23	*The Sorrows of Satan*	
Dec 8	*The Sign of the Cross*	Ben Greet Co
Jan 3-5	Claud Byng Musical and Speciality Company	

1898 St Mary's Hall

Jan 27	Annual Public Tea	PSA
Jan 31	A Dance	
Feb 2-3	*Humpty Dumpty*	Miss Jessie D'Alton Co

Feb 7	A Dance	
Feb 14	Annual Ball	Henley Town Cricket Club
Feb 28	A Dance	
Mar 7	A Dance	
Mar 14-15	*The Japanese Girl*	Mr Harold Perry's Co
Mar 31/Apr 1	*Cinderella*	Mr Fred Smith's Company
Apr 3	Violin Recital	Mr Fredalph Windeatt
Apr 6	Public Meeting	Henley and Nettlebed Conservative Assoc
Apr 11	Variety Entertainment	Mr WS Tanner Company
Apr 27	A Select Dance	
Jul 17	Distribution of Prizes	PSA
Sep 12-13	*Madcap Madge*	Miss Ivy Rivers & Company
Oct 20-22	Great Minstrel Troupe	Carl Howlett's Company
Oct 28-29	*Cole's Merry Folks* and a new Comic Operetta *The Wrong Man*	
Nov 17-19	*Merry Dick Whittington*	Miss Jessie D'Alton's Co

1899	**St Mary's Hall**	
Jan 5-6	*The Ladder of Life*	Miss Maggie Morton's Co
Jan 11	A Dramatic Entertainment	Church Tower Restoration Fund
Jan 23	*The Sign of the Cross*	Ben Greet Company
Feb 15	Illustrated lecture – *Khartoum at Last*	Mr Frederick Villiers
Mar 23	Maidenhead Minstrels and a humorous sketch *Black Justice*	
Apr 13-14	Henley Industrial and Artistic Exhibition	
Jul 30	Distribution of Prizes	PSA
Sep 14-16	*Our Boys*	Thomas Thorne Company
Oct 9	*The Private Secretary*	Edward Graham Falcon's Company
Nov 12-13	*The Three Musketeers*	Comedie Anglaise Company
Nov 25	*East Lynne*	Ben Greet Company
Dec 12-13	*The Money Spinner*	
Dec 18	Patriotic Concert	

1900	**St Mary's Hall**	
Jan 18	A Dance	
Jan 24	PSA Annual Tea and Great Public Meeting	
Feb 14-15	*Sinbad the Sailor*	GW Bowes Co
Feb 20	A Grand Evening Concert	Holy Trinity Church Choir
Apr 24	A Dance	
Apr 23	Patriotic Entertainment and a one-act play *Popping the Question*	
Apr 27	Animated Photographs of the war. Followed by Musical Entertainment.	G Goodwin Norton
May 17	Grand Evening Vocal and Instrumental Recital	Mr WE Weston
Jul 2	Mr Albert Chevalier's Recitals	
Sep 3-4	*A Pair of Spectacles and Caste*	Mr Russell Rosse Company

Oct 1	*Florodora*	JV Woods Company
Oct 10	*Living Pictures*	Mr G Egerton
Oct 26-27	*Charley's Aunt*	Mr WS Penley London Co
Nov 19-21	Speer's Grand Cinematograph and Variety Entertainment	

1901 St Mary's Hall

Jan 24	Distribution of Prizes	PSA
Jan 24-25	*Babes in the Wood*	Miss Jessie D'Anton Co
Feb 11-13	*Life in Our Navy*	West's Animated Photographs
Mar 11-12	Cole's Ventriloquial Recitals and Humerous Mimetic Entertainments with up-to-date Animated Pictures	Mr WH Speer Co
Apr 23	*Dandelions' Dodges* and *Ticklish Times*	
May 18	Rummage Sale	Parochial Fund
Jul 1	Mr Albert Chevalier's Recitals	
Aug 5	Grand Entertainment incorporating A Grand Baby Show	
Aug 26-27	*Beauty and the Beast*	Miss Jessie d'Anton Co
Sep 16-17	*The Mad Doctor*	International Operatic, Dramatic and Variety Co
Oct 3	Animated Pictures	Mr WF Jury
Nov 9	*The Second in Command*	Ben Greet Co
Nov 18-19	*Nell Gwynne*	Comedie Anglaise Co
Dec 6	*Belle of New York*	Ben Greet Co
Dec 31	*Aladdin and his Wonderful Lamp*	G Egerton Burnett Co

1902 St Mary's Hall

Jan 13	A Meeting and Entertainment with Animated Photographs	Primrose League
Feb 8	*The Magistrate*	
Mar 6	*The Famous Imperial Pierrots*	Bernard Stalay Co
Jun 6	Peace Thanksgiving Service	
Aug 7-8	*Uncle Tom's Cabin*	Josh Hybert Co
Sep 17	Moore and Burgess Minstrels	
Oct 10	*The Geisha*	Mr Mouillot Co
Oct 20	Meeting	PSA
Oct 29	*Floradora*	Ben Greet Co

1903 St Mary's Hall

Jan 9	*A Chinese Honeymoon*	George Dance's Co
Feb 16-17	*Are You a Mason?*	George Edwardes and Chas Frohman Co
Mar 27-28	Animated Pictures and Entertainment	
Aug 2	Meeting	PSA
	Note: From August 2nd the PSA met regularly every Sunday until the end of the year.	
Sep 15	*The Private Secretary*	Edward Graham-Falcon Company
Dec 30	*Quality Street*	Ben Greet Co

1904 St Mary's Hall

Jan 3	Meeting	PSA
Jan 7	*The Forty Thieves*	Egerton Burnett Co
Jan 10	Meeting	PSA
Jan 17	Meeting	PSA

Jan 24	Meeting	PSA
Jan 30	*Cynthia's Captive* and *True Colours* and *Atchi*	
Feb 7	Meeting	PSA

From week ending February 13th 1904, the building was known as Kenton Hall.

Feb 14	Meeting	PSA
Feb 16	*A Chinese Honeymoon*	Chas Macdonna Co
Apr 7	A Children's Entertainment	Remenham CU
Apr 12	Gymnastic Display	Church Institute Gymnastic Club
Apr 21	*A Country Girl*	Chas Macdonna Co
Aug 15	*The Indian Mutiny*	Maggie Morton Co
Oct 15	*Charley's Aunt*	WS Penley Co
Oct 22	*Cousin Kate*	Chas Macdonna Co
Dec 28	*Bo-peep's Picnic*	

1905	**Kenton Hall**	
Jan 8	Meeting	PSA
Apr 4	Gymnastic Display	Church Institute Gymnastic Club
Apr 24	Grand Concert	Henley Town Band
May 8	Rummage Sale	Henley Parochial Fund
Aug 30	*Sweethearts* and *The Kings Messenger* and *A Husband in Clover*	Amateur Production
Oct 9	*The Christian*	J Bannister Howard Co
Nov 4	*The Private Secretary*	Edward Graham-Falcon Co

1906	**Kenton Hall**	
Jan 15	*The Enchanted Glen*	
Apr 3	Gymnastic Display	Church Institute Gymnastic Club
Apr 18	Children's Entertainment	Miss M Wright
Apr 28	Rummage Sale	Henley Parochial Fund
Sep 28	*San Toy*	Robert Macdonald Co
Dec 6	A Benefit Concert for the Widow and Children of the late Charles Rawlings	
Dec 12-13	Jury's Imperial Animated Pictures	

1907	**Kenton Hall**	
Jan 18	*The Wishing Cap*	Arranged by Miss Honeysett
Jan 21-22	*Robinson Crusoe*	Chattell & Bowes Co
Feb 1	*The Silver King*	J Bannister Howard Co
Feb 22	*Bluebell in Fairyland*	Edward Graham Falcon Co
Oct 11	*The Earl and the Girl*	J Bannister Howard Co
Oct 30	Ellis's Great Clearance Sale	
Nov 6	*The Christian*	J Bannister Howard Co

1908	**Kenton Hall**	
Jan 7-8	*Cinderella*	Cecil Clayton Co
Jan 16	Entertainment and *Chiselling*	Amateur Production
Jan 20	*Dick Whittington and his Cat*	
Mar 11	Meeting and a one-act play *What Free Trade did for Bill*	Unionist and Tariff Reform Association
May 2	Rummage Sale	Henley Parochial Fund
Jul 22-23	*Saturday to Monday*	Miss Kemmis Co
Sep 28	*When Knights were Bold*	J Bannister Howard Co
Oct 2-3	*Aladdin and his Wonderful Lamp*	Miss Jessie D'Alton Co

Oct 8	Smoking Concert	Conservative and Tariff Reform Association
Nov 18	Love in Arcady	
1909	**Kenton Hall**	
Jan 14	Betty's Engagement	Amateur Production
Jan 18	Sinbad the Sailor	John A Thompson Company
Mar 24	Living Pictures Music by the Wargrave Amateur Orchestra	Society for the Propagation of the Gospel
Apr 21	Entertainment and Cinderella and the Glass Slipper and Nursery Rhyme Tableaux Music by the Wargrave Orchestra	Miss Ames & Mrs Brakspear
May 8	Rummage Sale	Henley Parochial Fund
May 22	Smoking Concert by NCOs and men of D Company, 4th Battalion Oxfordshire and Buckinghamshire Light Infantry	
Oct 12	East Lynne	Nevill Graham Co
Oct 25-30	Jury's Imperial Pictures A dash to the North Pole	
Dec 23-24	Red Riding Hood	Barrie & Barry Co
1910	**Kenton Hall**	
Mar 14	Dr Seaton's Grand National Animated Photos and Concert Party	
Mar 21-26	Dr Seaton's Grand National Animated Photos and Concert Party	
1911-1925	The Kenton Hall was not in use as a Hall or a Theatre	
1926	**Kenton Hall**	
May 3-5	Iolanthe	HRAODS

1927	**Kenton Hall**	
Apr 25-27	The Mikado	HRAODS
1928	There is no record of any production in this year	
1929	There is no record of any production in this year	
1930	**The Playhouse**	
Jan 28	The Tricking of Malvolio and The Rational Princess	The Ranger Players 2nd Henley Company
Apr 30/ May 1-3	Miss Hook of Holland	HRAODS
Oct 14-15	Dawn was Theirs	Thames Players
1931	**The Playhouse**	
Feb 2-4	A Damsel in Distress	HRAODS
Feb 6	Drama Festival	Oxfordshire Rural Community Council
Apr 8-9	In Saramede	The Rangers Players 2nd Henley Company
Jun 1-6	Lost Property	Barney Lando & Company
Jun 8-13	The Laugh Bowl	,,
Jun 21-23	Wanted – a Baby	,,
Jun 24-26	The House of Happenings	,,
Jun 29/Jul 4	Special Regatta Attraction	,,
Jul 6-11	Midnight Matinee – Mixed Salad	,,
Jul 13-18	The Super Tit-Bits	,,
Jul 20-25	Punch and Pep	,,
Jul 27	Something Good	BB Productions
Aug 3-8	Wide Awake (Variety)	Jose Brooks Presents

Aug 10-15	*Summer Stars*	Cecil Austin
Aug 17-22	*Cabaret Serenaders*	,,
Aug 24-29	*Hot Punch*	,,
Aug 31/ Sep 5	*Song and Harmony*	,,
Sep 7-12	*Stage Circus and Road Show*	,,
Sep 14-19	*Sauce* (Variety)	,,
Sep 21-26	*Stars of the Night*	,,
Sep 28/Oct 3	*The Fun Show*	,,
Oct 5-10	*Full Variety*	,,
Oct 12-17	*Vaudeville Times*	,,
Nov 9-10	*A Beggar on Horseback*	Frank Buckley and his No 1 Repertory Company
Nov 11-12	*A Peep behind the Scenes*	,,
Nov 13	*East Lynne*	,,
Nov 14	*A White Man's Way*	,,
Nov 16-17	*A College Girl's Romance*	,,
Nov 18-19	*Hindle Wakes*	,,
Nov 20	*My Husband's Future Wife*	,,
Nov 21	*The Death Trap*	,,
Nov 23-24	*Darby and Joan*	,,
Nov 25-26	*Caste*	,,
Nov 27	*A Daughter of the Regiment*	,,
Nov 28	*The Egyptian and The Woman*	,,

1932 The Playhouse

Jan 8-9	*A Summer in Paradise*	Under New Management
Apr 11-13	*The Middle Watch*	HRAODS
Jun 27/Jul 2	*The Man who ate the Popomack*	Group Theatre
Dec 20-22	*Tilly of Bloomsbury*	Henley Grammar School

1933 The Playhouse

Jan 25	*The Earthquake*	Reading Youth Group Players
Jan 27	*Drama Festival*	Oxford Rural Community Council
Feb 20-24	*The Yeomen of the Guard*	HRAODS
May 3	*A Great Entertainment*	Henley Parish Church
Dec 18-20	*Leave it to Psmith*	HRAODS

1934 The Playhouse

Feb 7-9	*Romeo and Juliet*	Henley Grammar School (The Periam Society)
Apr 25	*A Variety Entertainment*	Henley Senior C of E School assisted by public talent
Nov 28-30	*Hamlet*	Henley Grammar School
Dec 22	*A Murder has been Arranged*	

1935 The Playhouse

Jan 8-10	*Quality Street*	HRAODS

1936 The Playhouse

Sep 4	*Concord Follies*	
Sep 11	*Concord Follies*	
Sep 21-23	*Murder on the Second Floor*	County Repertory Players
Sep 24-26	*The Rotters*	,,
Sep 28-30	*Smilin' Thru'*	,,
Oct 1-3	*The House of Terror*	,,

Oct 5-7	Meet the Wife	County Repertory Players
Oct 8-10	A Bunch of Violets	,,
Oct 12-14	White Cargo	,,
Oct 15-17	Smouldering Fires	,,
Oct 19-21	The Chinese Bungalow	,,
Oct 22-24	The Ghost Train	,,
Oct 26-28	Up in Mabel's Room	,,
Oct 29-31	Young Woodley	,,
Nov 2-4	Common Clay	,,
Nov 5-7	Dracula	,,
Nov 9-11	At Dawn	,,
Nov 12-14	All Men are Liars	,,
Nov 16-18	Death Takes a Holiday	,,
Nov 19-21	While Parents Sleep	,,
Nov 23-25	Eliza Comes to Stay	,,
Nov 26-28	The Last Warning	,,
Nov 30	The Volcano – New play's first production – one night only	,,
Dec 1	While Parents Sleep – by special request	,,
Dec 2	Billy's Indiscretion – New play's first production – one night only	,,
Dec 3-5	Almost a Honeymoon	,,
Dec 7-9	Private Lives	,,
Dec 10-12	The Creaking Door	,,

1937 The Playhouse

Jan 4-6	Leah the Forsaken	County Repertory Players
Jan 7-9	Tainted Goods	,,
Jan 11-13	Three Women and a Man	,,
Jan 14-16	Sweeney Todd (by special request)	,,
Jan 18-20	Nearly Beloved, Women Must Weep and Mauru	,,
Jan 21-23	The Naughty Wife	,,
Jan 25-30	Her First Affair	Joseph Cunningham with the Zillah Bateman Players
Feb 1-6	The Shining Hour	,,
Feb 8-13	Love from a Stranger	,,
Feb 15-20	The Rainbow Girl	,,
Feb 22-27	The Face at the Window	,,
Mar 1-6	Ghosts	,,
Mar 8-13	Jane	A Brandon-Cremer and the Henley Repertory Players
Mar 15-20	The Crimson Crescent	,,
Mar 22-27	Maria Marten or The Murder in the Red Barn	,,
Mar 29-31	Hindle Wakes	,,
Apr 1-3	The Joan Danvers	,,
Apr 5-7	Ashamed of the Man She Married	,,
Apr 8-10	Over the Hill	,,
Apr 12-14	East Lynne (by special request)	,,
Apr 15-17	A Bill of Divorcement	,,
Apr 19-21	Autumn Fire	,,
Apr 22-24	The Fatal Wedding	,,
Apr 26-28	The Wrong Mr Smith	,,
Apr 29/May 1	Skittles	,,
May 3-5	The Black Moth	,,
May 6-8	Tilly of Bloomsbury	,,
May 10-12	Much Married	,,

May 13-15	*The Man from Toronto*	,,
May 17-19	*The Manx Man*	,,
May 20-22	*In the Soup*	,,
Sep 20-25	*Bats in the Belfry*	Matthew Forsyth and his Company
Sep 27/Oct 2	*Lovers Leap*	,,
Oct 4-9	*Night Must Fall*	,,
Oct 11-16	*The Late Christopher Bean*	,,
Oct 18-21	*It Pays to Advertise*	,,
Dec 27/Jan 1	*Turkey Time*	

1938 The Playhouse

Jan 3-8	*On the Spot* (Adults Only)	
Feb 22	Variety Entertainment in aid of Royal Berks Extension Fund	The Henley Townswomen's Guild
Mar 21-26	*Riverside Revels*	Raymond Bennett
Mar 28/Apr 2	,,	,,
Apr 4-9	,,	,,
Apr 11-16	,,	,,
Apr 18-23	,,	,,
Apr 27-30	*Iolanthe*	HRAODS

1939

Jan 30/Feb 4	*The Rollers*	Randall-Newall Players
Feb 6-11	*Double Error*	,,
Feb 13-18	*Miss Cinders*	,,
Feb 20-25	*Simple Simon's Baby*	,,
Feb 27/Mar 4	*Simple Simon's Baby*	,,
Apr 19th	Variety Concert	Miss Ena Grossmith and her London Co

Apr 26-29	*The Arcadians*	HRAODS

The theatre is renamed The New Playhouse

May 27/Jun 3	*Dangerous Corner*	Sidney Foster and The Henley Players (Formerly London Players)
Jun 5-10	*Hay Fever*	,,
Jun 12-17	*The Two Mrs Carrolls*	,,
Jun 19-24	*Pygmalion*	,,
Jun 26/Jul 1	*Yes and No*	,,
Jul 3-5	*Canaries Sometimes Sing*	,,
Jul 6-8	*Springtime for Henry*	,,
Jul 10-15	*Escape Me Never*	,,
Jul 17-22	*Lord Richard in the Pantry*	,,
Jul 24-29	*The Cat and the Canary*	,,
Jul 31/Aug 5	*The Sport of Kings*	,,
Aug 7-12	*The Late Christopher Bean*	,,
Aug 14-19	*Behold We Live*	,,
Aug 21-26	*The Importance of Being Earnest*	,,
Aug 28/Sep 2	*Yellow Sands*	,,

Theatre closed September 3rd due to outbreak of war re-opened 11th September 1939.

Sep 11-16	*The Maitlands*	,,
Sep 18-23	*Tell me the Truth*	,,
Sep 25-30	*Britannia of Billingsgate*	,,
Oct 2-7	*George and Margaret*	,,
Oct 10-14	*Candida*	,,
Oct 16-21	*Laburnum Grove*	,,
Oct 23-28	*Eliza Comes to Stay*	,,
Oct 30/Nov 4	*Dusty Ermine*	,,

Date	Play	Company
Nov 6-11	The First Mrs Fraser	Sydney Foster & the Henley Players
Nov 13-18	Mr Wu	,,
Nov 20-25	The Dominant Sex	,,
Nov 27/Dec 2	Orchids for Two	,,
Dec 4-9	Lot's Wife	,,
Dec 11-16	'Art an' Mrs Bottle	,,
Dec 26/Jan 13	Dick Whittington and his Cat	,,

1940 — The New Playhouse

Date	Play	Company
Jan 8-13	Dick Whittington and his Cat	Sydney Foster & the Henley Players
Jan 15-20	Night Must Fall	,,
Jan 22-27	The Spot on the Sun	,,
Jan 29/Feb 3	Autumn Crocus	,,
Feb 5-10	Gaslight	,,
Feb 12-17	The Bread Winner	,,
Feb 19-24	Man and Superman	,,
Feb 26/Mar 2	French Without Tears	,,
Mar 4-9	But Ladies First	,,
Mar 11-16	Eden End	,,
Mar 18-23	Outward Bound	,,
Mar 25-30	Honeymoon	,,
Apr 1-6	The Queen was in the Parlour	,,
Apr 8-13	Suspect	,,
Apr 15-20	While Parents Sleep	,,
Apr 22-27	The Barton Mystery	,,
Apr 29/May 4	By Candlelight	,,
May 6-11	Sixteen	,,
May 13-18	Goodness, How Sad	,,
May 20-25	Fresh Fields	,,
May 27/Jun 1	The Barretts of Wimpole Street	,,
Jun 3-8	Love from a Stranger	,,
Jun 10-15	Private Lives	,,
Jun 17-22	Mr Pimm Passes By	,,
Jun 24-29	Almost a Honeymoon	,,
Jul 1-6	Half Holiday	,,
Jul 8-13	The Rotters	,,
Jul 15-20	Sarah Simple	,,
Jul 22-27	Petticoat Influence	,,
Jul 29/Aug 3	Flat to Let	,,
Aug 5-10	Lovers Leap	,,
Aug 12-17	Cat's Cradle	,,
Aug 19-24	To See Ourselves	,,
Aug 26-31	The Naughty Wife	,,
Sep 2-7	Peg O' My Heart	,,
Sep 9-14	Important People	,,
Sep 16-21	Cornelius	,,
Sep 23-28	Ariadne	,,
Sep 30	Tonight at 8	
Oct 4	Hands across the Sea, Fumed Oak, Ways and Means	
Oct 7-12	If Four Walls Told	,,
Oct 14-19	Robert's Wife	,,
Oct 21-26	Ambrose Applejohn's Adventure	,,
Oct 28/Nov 2	Uneasy Living	,,
Nov 4-9	Wuthering Heights	,,
Nov 11-16	Winter Sunshine	,,
Nov 18-23	I'll Leave it to You	,,
Nov 25-30	The Man from Toronto	,,
Dec 2-7	Children to Bless You	,,

| Dec 9-14 | Room for Two | ,, |
| Dec 16/Jan 11 | Robinson Crusoe | ,, |

1941 — The New Playhouse

Feb 3-8	French Without Tears	Sidney Foster and the Henley Players
Feb 17-22	George and Margaret	,,
Feb 24/Mar 1	Arms and the Man	,,
Mar 3-8	Rebecca	,,
Mar 10-15	The Unfair Sex	,,
Mar 17-22	The Young Idea	,,
Mar 24-29	Five Aces	,,
Mar 31/Apr 5	The Shining Hour	,,
Apr 12-19	A little Bit of Fluff	,,
Apr 21-26	The Two Mrs Carrolls	,,
Apr 28/May 3	Lord Babs	,,
May 5-10	The Joan Danvers	,,
May 12-17	A Murder has been Arranged	,,
May 19-24	Full House	,,
May 25	Grand Variety Concert with Military Band	
May 26-31	Dangerous Corner	,,
Jun 2-7	The Wind and the Rain	,,
Jun 9-14	The Good Young Man	,,
Jun 16-21	Third Party Risk	,,
Jun 23-28	Rope	,,
Jun 30/Jul 5	Baby Mine	,,
Jul 7-12	Payment Deferred	,,
Jul 14-19	Artificial Silk	,,
Jul 21-26	Thunder in the Air	,,
Jul 28/Aug 2	Exeunt the Dictators by JB Hill (World Première)	,,
Aug 4-9	Painted Sparrows	,,
Aug 11-16	Fever	,,
Aug 18-23	The Chinese Bungalow	,,
Aug 25-30	All the King's Horses	,,
Sep 1-6	Mystery at Greenfingers	,,
Sep 8-13	Spring Meeting	,,
Sep 15-20	Intrigue	,,
Sep 22-27	The Magic Cupboard	,,
Sep 29/Oct 4	The Walk Alone	,,
Oct 6-11	The Patsy	,,
Oct 13-18	Black Limelight	,,
Oct 20-25	Punch Without Judy	,,
Oct 27/Nov 1	None So Blind	,,
Nov 3-8	Murder Party	,,
Nov 10-15	The Wrong Number	,,
Nov 17-22	It's a Boy	,,
Nov 24-29	The Sacred Flame	,,
Dec 1-6	A School for Husbands	,,
Dec 8-13	While Parents Sleep	,,
Dec 24/Jan 10	Cinderella	,,

1942 — The New Playhouse

Jan 10	Cinderella	Sydney Foster and the Henley Players
Jan 20-24	Night Lights (an intimate revue)	
Jan 26-31	Night Lights (Change of programme)	,,
Feb 2-7	Night Lights (Change of programme)	,,

Feb 9-14	Ladies in Retirement	Sydney Foster and the Henley Players
Feb 16-21	Charity begins...	,,
Feb 23-29	Once a Gentleman	,,
Mar 2-7	Time and the Conways	,,
Mar 9-14	Dear Brutus	,,
Mar 16-21	Indoor Fireworks	,,
Apr 5-11	Death takes a Holiday	,,
Apr 20-25	Bats in the Belfry	,,
Apr 20-25	The Eternal Spring	,,
Apr 27/May 2	The Way Things Happen	,,
May 4-9	The Truth About Blayds	,,
May 11-16	The Dover Road	,,
May 18-30	Rain	,,
May 25-30	The Last of Mrs Cheyney	,,
Jun 1-6	Billeted	,,
Jun 8-13	Musical Chairs	,,
Jun 15-20	Devonshire Cream	,,
Jun 22-27	Meet the Wife	,,
Jul 13-18	Nite-Lites (an intimate revue)	,,
Jul 20-25	Nite-Lites (Change of programme)	,,
Jul 27/Aug 1	Why Worry (a revue)	,,
Aug 3-8	Holiday at Home (a revue)	,,
Aug 10-15	So What (a revue)	,,
Aug 17-22	Musical Cocktails (a revue)	,,
Aug 24-29	Cheerio (a revue)	,,
Nov 9-14	The Marvellous History of St Bernard	Playhouse Theatre Club
Nov 17-21	Jam Today	Sydney Foster and the Henley Players
Nov 23-28	Why Not Tonight	,,
Nov 30/Dec 5	French for Love	,,
Dec 7-12	Love in a Mist	,,
Dec 14-19	On Approval	,,
Dec 21-25	Springtime for Henry	,,
Dec 27/Jan 2	Eliza Comes to Stay	,,

1943   **The New Playhouse**

Jan 4-9	The Case of Lady Camber	Sydney Foster's Henley Players
Jan 11-16	Quinneys	,,
Jan 18-23	The Astonished Ostrich	,,
Jan 25-30	The Family Upstairs	,,
Feb 1-6	Glass Houses	,,
Feb 8-13	A Bunch of Violets	,,
Mar 8-13	Variety	Sydney Foster presents
Mar 22-27	Russian Ballet de la jeunesse anglaise	Sydney Foster presents
Apr 26/May 1	Tainted Goods	,,
Jun 7-12	The Circle	Miles Bryan by arrangement with Sydney Foster presents
Jun 14-19	Fresh Fields	,,
Jun 21-26	Night Must Fall	,,
Jun 28/Jul 3	Hay Fever	,,
Jul 5-10	Tell me the Truth	,,
Aug 2-7	Blithe Spirit	Sydney Foster presents
Aug 9-14	Fallen Angels	Sydney Foster presents The Chelsea Players
Aug 16-21	Fallen Angels retained for another week	,,

Aug 23-28	Gas Light	,,
Aug 30/Sep 4	The Wind and the Rain	,,
Sep 6-11	The Bill of Divorcement	,,
Sep 13-18	Quiet Wedding	,,
Sep 20-25	The Late Christopher Bean	,,
Sep 27/Oct 2	The Rotters	,,
Oct 4-9	Good Men Sleep at Home	,,
Oct 11-16	Dead Man's Guest	,,
Oct 18-23	You Never Can Tell	,,
Oct 25-30	I Killed the Count	,,
Nov 1-6	On the Spot	,,
Nov 8-13	Mixed Doubles	,,
Nov 15-20	The Case of the Frightened Lady	,,
Nov 22-27	Ghosts	,,
Nov 29/Dec 4	Oliver Twist	,,
Dec 6-11	Bishops Move	,,
Dec 27/Jan 8	Babes in the Wood	,,

1944 The New Playhouse

Feb 24 & 25	Dancing and Dramatic Entertainment in aid of the Henley prisoner-of-war Fund	Miss Dorothy Greenhill
Feb 28/Mar 4	Bella Donna	Sidney Foster and the Chelsea Players
Mar 6-11	The Fur Coat	,,
Mar 13-18	Dr Brent's Household	,,
Mar 20-25	Goodness, How Sad	,,
Mar 27-Apr 1	Left to Chance	,,
Apr 10-15	She Stoops to Conquer	Sydney Foster and the Town and Country Theatre
Apr 17-22	Lottie Dundas	,,
Apr 24-29	Not for Publication	,,
May 1-6	They Came to a City	,,
May 8-13	Rebecca	,,
May 15-20	Hay Fever	,,
May 22-27	Pygmalion	,,
May 29/Jun 3	French Without Tears	,,
Jun 5-10	The Shining Hour	,,
Jun 12-17	East Lynne	The Morlet Theatre Co
Jun 19-24	On the Spot	Town and Country Theatre
Jun 26/Jul 1	Blithe Spirit	,,
Jul 3-8	On Approval	,,
Jul 10-15	The Importance of Being Earnest	,,
Jul 17-22	The Constant Wife	,,
Jul 24-29	The Corn is Green	,,
Jul 31/Aug 5	Rookery Nook	,,
Aug 7-12	Pride and Prejudice	,,
Aug 14-19	Watch on the Rhine	,,
Aug 21-26	Jeannie	,,
Aug 28/Sep 3	Arms and the Man	,,
Sep 4-9	Tony Draws a Horse	,,
Sep 11-16	Black Limelight	,,
Sep 18-23	Guilty	,,
Sep 25-30	The Old Foolishness	,,
Oct 2-7	George and Margaret	,,
Oct 9-14	Old Acquaintance	,,
Oct 16-21	The Light of Heart	,,
Oct 23-28	Mr Bolfry	,,
Oct 30/Nov 4	Mademoiselle	,,

Nov 6-11	Candida	Town and Country Theatre
Nov 13-18	Tonight at 8.30 Red Peppers, Fumed Oak, Hands across the Sea	,,
Nov 20-25	Night Must Fall	,,
Nov 27/Dec 2	Mary Rose	,,
Dec 4-9	No Time for Comedy	,,
Dec 11-16	The Springtime of Others	,,
Dec 26/Jan 6	Aladdin and his Wonderful Lamp	,,

1945 The New Playhouse

Jan 8-13	Charley's Aunt	Town and Country Theatre Ltd
Jan 15-20	Look Alive	,,
Jan 22-27	Jane Steps Out	,,
Jan 29/Feb 3	Sixteen	,,
Feb 5-10	Sarah Simple	,,
Feb 12-17	Acacia Avenue	,,
Apr 16-21	Nell Gwynne	Sydney Foster and the Henley Repertory Co
Apr 16-21	Love from a Stranger	,,
Apr 23-28	I Lived with You	,,
Apr 30/May 5	Spring Cleaning	,,
May 7-12	First Night	,,
May 14-19	The Druids Rest	,,
May 21-26	Anna Christie	,,
May 28/Jun 2	Springtime for Henry	,,
Jun 4-9	Russian Ballet	Lydia Kyash Coy
Jun 11-16	Bird in Hand	Henley Repertory Co
Jun 18-23	Claudia	,,
Jun 25-30	Three-Cornered Moon	,,
Jul 2-7	The House of Jeffreys	,,
Jul 9-14	Nell Gwynne	,,
Jul 16-21	The Private Secretary	,,
Jul 23-28	The Shining Hour	,,
Jul 30/Aug 4	Give Me Yesterday	,,
Aug 6-11	Saloon Bar	,,
Aug 13-18	Above repeated due to phenomenal success	
Aug 20-25	Arms and the Man	,,
Aug 27/Sep 1	Just Married	,,
Sep 3-8	They Fly by Twilight	,,
Sep 10-15	Above repeated due to phenomenal success	
Sep 17-22	The Gentlemanly Thing	Full cast of West End Artists
Sep 24-29	The Man with the Load of Mischief	Henley Repertory Co
Oct 1-6	Flare Path	,,
Oct 8-13	Laura	,,
Oct 15-20	The Mollusc	,,
Oct 29/Nov 3	A Soldier for Christmas	Sidney Foster presents the Lionel Westlake Company
Nov 5-10	Black Swans	,,
Nov 12-17	To-morrow's Eden	,,
Nov 19-24	Ann	,,
Dec 10-15	Squaring the Triangle	RAF Medmenham Rep Co
Dec 24	Humpty Dumpty CANCELLED	Sydney Foster presents

Dec 31/Jan 5	Babes in the (Kentucky) Wood	Sydney Foster & Ron Ronson

1946 — The New Playhouse

Jan 7-12	The Renowned Victory Follies Revue	Yat Sen & Williams present
Jan 14-19	Anglo-Russian Ballet	Latisha Browne
Jan 21-26	Cinderella	
Feb 4-9	Murder without Crime CANCELLED	
Feb 11-16	Murder without Crime	Entire London Co from the Lindsay Theatre
May 28/Jun 1	By Candle Light	Yvonne Le Dain with Henley Theatre Trust
Jun 4-8	The Violent Friends	,,
Jun 10-15	The Long Mirror	,,
Jun 18-22	Parisienne	,,
Jun 25-29	While the Sun Shines	,,
Jul 2-6	French for Love	,,
Jul 9-13	The Dream Again	,,
Jul 16-20	The First Mrs Fraser	,,
Jul 23-27	Fit for Heroes Nobility in a Portal House	,,
Jul 30/Aug 3	One Woman	Yvonne Le Dain
Aug 5-10	Peg O' My Heart	Yvonne Le Dain with Henley Theatre Trust
Aug 13-17	Gas Light	,,
Aug 20-24	Mr Pim Passes By	,,
Aug 27-31	Fresh Fields	,,
Sep 3-7	Pink String and Sealing Wax	,,
Sep 10-14	Love in a Mist	,,
Sep 17-21	On Approval	,,
Sep 24-28	Mrs Moonlight	,,
Oct 1-5	Laburnum Grove	,,
Oct 8-12	The Corn is Green	,,
Oct 15-19	Hay Fever	,,
Oct 22-26	Dangerous Corner	,,
Oct 29/Nov 2	The Temptations of Anthony	,,
Nov 5-9	Meet the Wife	,,
Nov 12-16	It's a Boy	,,
Nov 19-23	Eliza Comes to Stay	,,
Nov 26-30	Good Morning Bill!	,,
Dec 3-7	The Magic Cupboard	,,
Dec 26/Jan 11	Beauty and the Beast	,,

1947 — The New Playhouse

Apr 7-12	The Pied Piper	,,
Apr 15-19	The Barretts of Wimpole Street	,,
Apr 22-26	The Mollusc	,,
Apr 29/May 2	Law and Disorder	,,
May 6-10	Granite	,,
May 13-17	Canaries Sometimes Sing	,,
May 20-24	Flare Path	,,
May 26-30	Blithe Spirit	,,
Jun 3-7	They Fly by Twilight	,,
Jun 10-14	Old Acquaintance	,,
Jun 19-21	Macbeth	,,
Aug 4-9	Pygmalion	,,
Aug 12-16	Robert's Wife	,,
Aug 19-23	French Without Tears	,,
Aug 26-30	The Gleam	,,
Sep 2-6	Arsenic and Old Lace	,,

Sep 9-13	*Private Lives*	Yvonne Le Dain with Henley Theatre Trust
Sep 16-20	*The Dumb Wife of Cheapside* and *Coals of Fire*	,,
Sep 26/Oct 4	*Quality Street*	,,
Oct 7-9	*Arms and the Man*	,,
Dec 26	*The Sleeping Beauty* CANCELLED due to ill health of Miss le Dain	,,

1948	**The New Playhouse**	
Jan 6-10	*John Wright's Marrionettes*	Henley Theatre Trust In Assoc with the Friends of the Playhouse
May 6, 7 & 8	*The Yellow Jacket*	Yvonne Le Dain
May 17-22	*Jane Steps Out*	Henley Theatre Trust In Assoc with the Arts Council of GB
Jun 1-5	*An Inspector Calls*	,,
Nov 18-20	*You Never Can Tell*	Thames Valley All Professional Theatre Co in Assoc with the Arts Council
Dec 2-4	*The Guinea Pig*	,,
Dec 16-18	*Christmas in the Market Place*	,,
Dec 27/Jan 15	*Cinderella*	,,

1949	**The New Playhouse**	
Jan 27-29	*The Sacred Flame*	,,
Feb 10-12	*Tomorrow's Child*	,,
Feb 24-26	*Power Without Glory*	,,
Mar 10-12	*The Dover Road*	,,
Mar 24-26	*Rebecca*	,,
Apr 7-9	*Tobias and the Angel*	,,
Apr 21-23	*While Sun Shines*	,,
Jun 29-Jul 2	*John Wright's Marrionettes*	,,
Oct 22	*Mary and Variety and The Thirteenth Fairy*	Ami M Bhalsey
Oct 24-29	*Midget Town Marvels*	John Lester
Dec 26-31	*Three farces for Christmas Entertainment*	The Mobile Theatre

1950	**The New Playhouse**	
Jan 9-21	*Babes in the Wood*	Thames Valley Theatre Trust
Jan 23-28	*Fly Away, Peter*	Tuska Theatre Co
Jan 30/Feb 4	*The Importance of being Earnest*	,,
Feb 6-11	*The Chiltern Hundreds*	,,
Feb 16-18	*Robin Hood*	HRODS
Feb 20-25	*Maria Marten or The Murder in the Red Barn*	Tuska Theatre Company
Feb 27/Mar 4	*Present Laughter*	,,
Mar 6-11	*A Murder Has Been Arranged*	,,
Mar 13-18	*Bird in Hand*	,,
Mar 20-25	*The Full House*	,,
Mar 27/Apr 1	*Mr Bolfry*	,,
Apr 3-8	*Murder in the Cathedral*	,,
Apr 10-15	*When We Are Married*	,,
Apr 17-22	*The Playboy of the Western World*	,,
Apr 24-29	*High Temperature*	,,
May 1-6	*Whiteoaks*	,,
May 8-13	*Blithe Spirit*	,,
May 15-20	*As You Like It*	,,
May 22-27	*The Girl Who Couldn't Quite*	,,
May 29/Jun 3	*Rookery Nook*	,,

Jun 5-10	Our Town	,,
Jun 12-17	Little Lambs Eat Ivy	,,
Jun 19-24	The Letter	,,
Jun 26/Jul 1	Young Wives Tale	,,
Jul 3-8	The Drunkard	,,
Jul 10-15	Yes and No	,,
Jul 17-22	The Man from the Ministry	,,
Jul 24-29	French Without Tears	,,
Jul 31/Aug 5	The Shining Hour	,,
Aug 7-12	Born Yesterday	,,
Aug 14-19	Duet for Two Hands	,,
Aug 21-26	See How They Run	,,
Aug 29/Sep 2	Fools Rush In	,,
Sep 4-9	Heaven and Charing Cross	,,
Sep 11-16	Miranda	,,
Sep 18-23	Ten Little Niggers	,,
Sep 25-30	Why Men Leave Home	,,
Oct 2-7	Claudia, Claudia	,,
Oct 9-14	The Green Bay Tree	,,
Oct 16-21	The Man in Possession	,,
Oct 23-28	Easy Money	,,
Oct 30/Nov 4	The Eagle has Two Heads	,,
Nov 6-11	Private Lives	,,
Nov 13-18	The Ghost Train	,,
Nov 20-25	The Foolish Gentlewoman	,,
Nov 27/Dec 2	Mary Rose	,,
Dec 4-9	A Soldier for Christmas	,,
Dec 11-16	A Doll's House	,,
Dec 18-23	The Case of the Frightened Lady	,,
Dec 26-Jan 6	Jack and the Beanstalk	,,

1951	**The New Playhouse**	
Jan 10-13	Mother Goose	HRAODS
Mar 26-31	Hay Fever	Tuska Theatre Co
Apr 2-7	The Shop at Sly Corner	,,
Apr 9-14	The Lady from Edinburgh	,,
Apr 16-21	The Wind and the Rain	,,
Apr 23-28	George and Margaret	,,
Apr 30/May 5	Pygmalion	,,
May 7-12	The Happiest days of your Life	,,
May 14-19	Castle in the Air	,,
May 28-Jun 2	Bonaventure	,,
Jun 4-9	Murder at the Vicarage	,,
Jun 11-16	Spring Meeting	,,
Jun 18-23	Tons of Money	,,
Jun 25-30	Love in Albania	,,
Jul 2-7	Love in a Mist	,,
Jul 9-14	Lovers' Leap	,,
Jul 16/Oct 16	**Theatre closed**	
	Re-opened as The Kenton Theatre	
Oct 16-20	The Glass Menagerie	Kenton Theatre Management
Oct 23-27	September Tide	,,
Oct 30-Nov 3	Fallen Angels	,,
Nov 6-10	A Sleep of Prisoners	,,
Nov 27-Dec 1	Regatta Day	,,
Dec 26-Jan 6	The Beggar Prince – matinees only On Approval – evenings only	,,

1952	**The Kenton Theatre**	
Jan 8-12	Laburnum Grove	The Kenton Theatre Co

Jan 15-19	*Who Goes There*	The Kenton Theatre Co
Jan 22-28	*Captain Carvallo*	,,
Jan 29/Feb 2	*A Streetcar Named Desire*	,,
Feb 5-9	*Old Acquaintance*	,,
Feb 12-16	*Sweeney Todd*	,,
Feb 19-23	*A Village Wooing* and *A Phoenix too frequent*	,,
Feb 24/Mar 1	*Jinny Morgan*	,,
Mar 4-8	*The Respectable Prostitute* Preceded by *The Tinker's Wedding*	,,
Mar 13-15	*Love on the Dole*	The Henley Players
Mar 18-22	*Victoria Regina*	Kenton Theatre Co
Mar 25-29	*Wuthering Heights*	,,
Apr 1-5	*Tonight at 8.30 – Fumed Oak, Still Life, Ways and Means*	,,
Apr 8-12	*The Way of the Cross* and *The Resurrection*	,,
Apr 14-19	*Charley's Aunt*	,,
Apr 22-26	*Traveller's Joy*	,,
Apr 30/May 3	*The Mikado*	HRAODS
May 6-10	*The Cocktail Party*	Kenton Theatre Co
May 13-27	*White Cargo*	,,
May 20-24	*Lot's Wife*	,,
May 27-31	*Symphonique Pastorale*	,,
Jun 2-7	*The Holy Terrors*	,,
Jun 10-14	*Don't Listen Ladies*	,,
Jun 17-21	*Antigone*	,,
Jun 25-29	*Regatta Day*	,,
Jun 30/Jul 4	*Nine O'clock Revue*	,,
Jul 21/Aug 2	*Ballet*	John Cranko Co
Sep 30/Oct 4	*Lilac Time*	
Nov 6-8	*Fresh Fields*	The Henley Players
Dec 14	*A Recital of Music and Poetry*	Kenton Theatre Co
Dec 20	*Alice Through the Looking Glass Ballet*	,,

1953	**The Kenton Theatre**	
Feb 12-14	*Night Must Fall*	The Henley Players
Feb 26-28	*Blithe Spirit*	The Henley Players
Mar 17-21	*The Gondoliers*	HRAODS

1954	**The Kenton Theatre**	
Dec 9-11	*Queen Elizabeth Slept Here*	Joint Amateur Production
Dec 30/Jan 1	*Ballets Minerva*	Minerva Productions

1955	**The Kenton Theatre**	
Feb 18-19	*One Act Play Festival*	Oxfordshire Rural Community
Apr 20-23	*Floradora*	Henley Amateur Operatic Society
May 5	*Caste*	Caryl Jenner Mobile Theatre
May 13-14	*Fools Rush In*	Shiplake Players
May 18-20	*Playgoers* and *The Rose and Crown* and *Passion, Poison and Petrifaction*	South Oxfordshire County Drama Association
Jun 21-25	*Round the Bend* (Revue)	Kenton Players
Oct 13-15	*Heaven* and *Charing Cross*	The Henley Players
Oct 29	*Lace on her Petticoat*	Caryl Jenner Mobile Theatre
Nov 4-5	*Someone Waiting*	Shiplake Players

Nov 11	*Oxfordshire FWI Drama Festival*	
Dec 2-3	*Ladies in Waiting*	Kenton Players
Dec 9-10	*Present Laughter*	Peppard Drama Group

1956	**The Kenton Theatre**	
Jan 13	*Beauty and the Beast*	Caryl Jenner Mobile Theatre
Mar 15-17	*Thark*	The Henley Players
Mar 31	*An Inspector Calls*	Caryl Jenner Mobile Theatre
Mar 11-14	*Old Chelsea*	HAODS
Jun 19-23	*The Importance of Being Earnest*	Associated Counties Theatre Society
Jun 25-29	*Who's for Tennis* (Regatta Revue)	Oxford Revue Group
Jul 12-13	*Blithe Spirit*	RAF Benson Players
Oct 19	*Village Wooing* and *Candida*	The Phoenix Players
Oct 26	*The Burning Glass*	Caryl Jenner Mobile Theatre
Nov 2-3	*The Heiress*	Greys Players
Nov 16-17	*Golden Rain*	The Henley Players
Nov 23-24	*The Happy Marriage*	Shiplake Players
Nov 30/Dec 1	*Seeing Stars*	The Henley Catholic Dramatic Society

1957	**The Kenton Theatre**	
Jan 3-5	*Dear Brutus*	Peppard Drama Group
Feb 1	*Where the Heart Is*	Caryl Jenner Mobile Theatre
Feb 26	*One Act Play Festival*	Oxfordshire Rural Community Council
Mar 22-23	*Present Laughter*	Woodley Players
Mar 28-30	*Pink String and Sealing Wax*	The Henley Players
Apr 26-27	Eastern Area Finals of the National Festival of Community Drama	
May 1-4	*The Count of Luxembourg*	HAODS
May 23-25	*Asmodee*	Associated Counties Theatrical Society
Jun 18-22	*Ever Since Paradise*	,,
Jun 29/Jul 6	*Out of the Sun* (Revue)	Oxford Revue Group
Nov 13-16	*Castle in the Air*	Woodley Players
Nov 21-23	*It's Never too Late*	The Henley Players
Nov 27	Women's Institute Drama Festival	
Dec 6-7	*The Lengthening Shadow* POSTPONED	Henley Catholic Drama Club
Dec 13-14	*The Noble Spaniard*	Peppard Drama Group

1958	**The Kenton Theatre**	
Jan 31/Feb 1	*The Lengthening Shadow*	Henley Catholic Drama Club
Mar 15	Berkshire County Drama Festival	
Mar 21-23	*Antigone*	Shiplake Players
Apr 15-19	*Brigadoon*	HAODS
May 9-10	*All For Mary*	The Henley Players
Jun 28/Jul 5	*The Love of Four Colonels*	ACTS

1959	**The Kenton Theatre**	
Feb 4-7	*Sailor Beware*	The Henley Players
Mar 13-14	Berkshire County Drama Festival	
Mar 20-21	*Home Fires*	Shiplake Women's Institute
Mar 24	South Oxfordshire Youth Advisory Committee Area Drama Festival	
Apr 13-18	*The Student Prince*	HAODS

May 28-30	Two's Company or The Bear, The Cock and the Bull	The Kenton Players
Jun 12	Songs I Like to Sing	
Jun 28/Jul 3	One Over the Eight (Revue)	Worcester College Ruskins
Sep 30/Oct 3	Dry Rot	The Henley Players
Oct 14-17	General Selection	HAODS
Nov 28	WI Drama Festival	
Dec 3-5	Invitation to a Voyage and The Pool by the Dragon Gate	ACTS

1960 — The Kenton Theatre

Mar 9-12	The Love Match	The Henley Players
Mar 21	Drama Festival	Oxfordshire Youth Organisations
Apr 25-30	Oklahoma!	HAODS
May 24-28	The Rape of the Belt	ACTS
Jun 27/Jul 2	Next Time Yes (Revue)	Worcester College Buskins
Oct 18-22	My Three Angels	The Henley Players
Nov 9-12	Book of the Month	Henley Drama Group
Nov 23-26	The Seducer	Shiplake Players

1961 — The Kenton Theatre

Feb 18	Drama Festival	Oxfordshire Rural Community Council
Feb 27/28	Drama Festival	Oxfordshire Education Committee Youth Service
Mar 22-25	A Breath of Spring	Henley Drama Club
Apr 17-22	South Pacific	HAODS
Apr 27-29	Random Harvest	Bracknell Mummers
Jun 28/Jul 1	Ring Round the Moon	Worcester College Buskins
Oct 4-7	Sabrina Fair	HAODS
Oct 25-28	Separate Tables	Henley Drama Club

1962 — The Kenton Theatre

Jan 10-13	The Princess and the Swineherd	The Henley Players
Jan 14	A Night at the Opera (Film)	Kenton Theatre Arts Club
Feb 16-17	The Strong are Lonely	Culham College Players
Mar 3	Stars of Tomorrow	Jeanine Greville School
Mar 28-31	Witness for the Prosecution	Henley Drama Club
Apr 30/May 5	Carousel	HAODS
May 9-12	Heartbreak House	Tamesis Players
Nov 14-16	You can't take it with you	Henley Drama Club

1963 — The Kenton Theatre

Mar 13-16	Doctor in the House	The Henley Players
Apr 22-27	Annie Get Your Gun	HAODS
May 17	The Best of Laurel and Hardy	Kenton Theatre Arts Club

1964 Theatre Closed

1965 Theatre Closed

1966 Theatre Closed

1967 — The Kenton Theatre

Mar 20-23 and 25	Amphytrion 38	Oxford Playhouse Company
Apr 3-8	The Pajama Game	HAODS
Apr 13-15	The Way of the World	City of Oxford Theatre Guild

Apr 16	Dennis Matthews (Pianist)	Henley Concerts	
Apr 17-22	Dear Liar		
Apr 27-29	A Funny Kind of Evening with David Kossoff		
Apr 30	A Teach-In	The River Thames Soc	
May 1-2	The Hostage	City of Oxford Link Theatre	
May 4-6	Oxfordshire Festival of Drama 1967 Finals		
May 8-13	Harlequin Ballet	Yvonne Meyer & Ivan Dragadze Co	
May 18-20	Vanity Fair	Sylvia Read & William Fry	
May 21	Gilbert and Sullivan	John Heddle Nash	
May 25-27	Red Noses for Me	Charles Lewsons	
May 29/Jun 3	Job for the Boy	John Inman & Barry Howard	
Jun 4-10	The Devils	County Drama Assoc	
Jun 15-17	The Importance of being Oscar	Michael MacLiammoir	
Jun 19, 20, 24	The Sparkle of Noel Coward	Hannah Watt & Roderick I Lovell	
Jun 21-23	The Kreutzer Sonata	,,	
Jun 25	As the Poet Sees It	Gladys Cooper, Celia Johnson	
Jun 26/Jul 1	The Reluctant Debutante	Hubert Woodward in association Robin Alexander & Cameron Mackintosh	
Jul 3-8	Dial M for Murder	,,	
Jul 11-15	Five Finger Exercise	,,	
Jul 17-22	The Chiltern Hundreds	,,	
Jul 24-29	The Knack	,,	
Aug 2-5	Beatrice Cenci		
Oct 2-7	Salad Days	HAODS	
Oct 10-21	Anatol	Zack Matalon Co	
Oct 24/Nov 4	The Night of January 16th	,,	
Nov 7-18	The Little Hut	,,	
Nov 21-25	Hay Fever	The Henley Players	
Nov 28/Dec 9	Exiles	Conrad Phillips & Zack Matalon	
Dec 12-23	The Fantasticks		
Dec 26/Jan 6	Let Down Your Hair		

1968 — The Kenton Theatre

Jan 8-13	To Dorothy, a Son	Zack Matalon Co
Jan 22-27	Picnic in Town	,,
Feb 24	Folk Entertainment	Len Harman
Mar 16	The World of Brecht	Oxford Playhouse Company
Mar 2	Folk Entertainment	Len Harman
Apr 2-6	The Imaginary Invalid and The Laboratory	The Henley Players
Apr 9-11	Mandragola	Oxford Theatre Guild
Apr 22-27	How to Succeed in Business Without Really Trying	HAODS
May 18	Folk Entertainment	Len Harman
Jun 15	Folk Entertainment	Len Harman
Jul 8-13	Annabella	Trinity Players
Jul 14	Singing for Pleasure	Jamie Fowler
Aug 2/3	Vodka and Tonic	Under 25 Players
Sep 7	Folk Entertainment	Len Harman
Sep 24-28	Romeo and Juliet	Henley Link Theatre

Oct 2-4	Funny Kind of Evening with *David Kossoff*	
Oct 5	Folk Entertainment	Len Harman
Oct 9-12	The Sleeping Prince	HAODS
Oct 19	Les Musicales	Beryl Lee
Nov 19-23	Black Chiffon	The Henley Players
Nov 30	Folk Entertainment	Len Harman
Dec 13/14	Poetry and Music	John Fairfax, John Moat and Paul Roche
Dec 16-20	Twice Five is Three (A revue)	HM productions

1969 The Kenton Theatre

Jan 8-11	Rumplstiltskin	The Grimm Players
Jan 12	Cheese and Wine Party	Kenton Theatre Club
Jan 27/Feb 1	Under Milk Wood	HM Productions
Feb 3-8	The Promise	,,
Feb 10-12	Rapunzel	Little Angels Marionette Theatre
Feb 17-22	Next Time I'll Sing to You	HM Productions
Feb 24	The Private Ear & The Public Eye	,,
Mar 3-8	Little Malcolm and his Struggle	,,
Mar 9	Special Cabaret (for Theatre Club Members and Guests)	
Mar 19-22	Uncle Vanya	The Henley Players
Mar 26-29	Antigone	Henley Grammar School
Apr 14-19	Guys and Dolls	HAODS
May 17	Three-Act County Drama Festival – Final	
May 19-24	The Hanging Wood (World Premier)	HM Productions
May 27-31	Loot	,,
Jun 3-7	Under Milk Wood	,,
Jun 17-21	Look Back in Anger	,,
Jun 24-29	Waiting for Godot	,,
Jul 1-7	Lysistrata Late Night Revue 10.30pm	,,
Jul 9-12	Boeing-Boeing	HAODS
Jul 14-19	Old Time Music Hall	Michael Holden
Jul 28/Aug 1	Heartbreak House	HM Productions
Sep 29/Oct 4	Bell, Book and Candle	The Holborn Theatre Co
Oct 6-11	The Boy Friend	HAODS
Oct 29/Nov 1	Clyde-O-Scope	Gordon Clyde
Nov 10-12	Marionette Theatre	John Wright
Nov 17-22	Private Lives	The Holborn Theatre Co
Nov 25-26	Ballet	London Contemporary Dance Group
Nov 27-28	Curtain Up	The Oxford Playhouse Co
Dec 4-7	The Crucible	The Henley Players
Dec 13	Jazz Evening	1066 Jazzmen
Dec 26-31	The Enchanted Well	John Reilly

1970 The Kenton Theatre

Jan 7-10	Tom Piper (Premier)	The Grimm Players
Feb 24-28	The Pleasure of his Company	HAODS
Mar 16-21	The Night I Chased the Women CANCELLED	David Gordon Productions
Apr 6-11	West Side Story	HAODS
Apr 22-25	Relatively Speaking	Shiplake Players

May 2	A Day of Drama	Oxfordshire County Festival
	The Killing of Sister George	Chinnor Players
	Romanoff and Juliet	Thame Players
May 5-9	*Spring and Port Wine*	The Henley Players
May 11-16	*Oliver*	The Unity Players of Slough
Jun 27	*Say Who You Are*	The Wick Players
Jul 2/3	*Old Tyme Music Hall*	The Unity Players of Slough
Sep 21-25	*The Pajama Game*	Reading Amateur Theatre Society
Oct 11-14	*Finian's Rainbow*	HAODS
Nov 11-14	*An Evening of Comedy: The Bald Prima Donna* (Black Comedy)	The Henley Players
Dec 13	*Singing for Pleasure*	HAODS

1971 — The Kenton Theatre

Jan 2	*Recital*	Jonathan Beacher ('cello) Frank Mulder (Piano)
Jan 13-16	*Cinderella*	
Feb 16-20	*Annabelle Third Floor* (World Premier)	The Grimm Players
Feb 24-27	*Called to the Bar*	HAODS
Mar 10-13	*The Killing of Sister George*	The Henley Players
Mar 15-20	*Carousel*	Reading Amateur Theatrical Society
Mar 24 & 26	*Il Trovatore*	The Misbourne Opera Group
Mar 27	*It's a Pleasure*	Kenton Theatre Saturday Morning Children's Group
Mar 31	Fashion Show	Facys
Apr 16-24	*My Fair Lady*	HAODS
May 5-8	*Plaza Suite*	Shiplake Players
May 23	*Pleasure and Repentance* An evening of Poetry with Music	The Henley Players
Jun 23-26	*Ring Round the Moon*	South Oxon Branch County Drama Assoc
Jun 28/Jul 3	*Strictly Confidential* Pre-London production of New Musical	Martin L Tyme presents
Jul 14-17	*The Lion in Winter*	HAODS
Sep 29/Oct 2	*Sganarelle and The Real Inspector Hound*	The Henley Link Theatre
Oct 5-9	*Half a Sixpence*	Reading Amateur Theatrical Society
Oct 18-23	*The Gondoliers*	HAODS
Nov 27	*Cinderella*	Henley Children's Theatre Group
Dec 2-4	*Wait Until Dark*	The Henley Players
Dec 18	*Dick Whittington*	Henley Children's Theatre Group

1972 — The Kenton Theatre

Mar 7-11	*Ernani*	Misbourne Opera Group
Mar 23-25	*Everything in the Garden*	The Henley Players
Apr 7-15	*Little Me*	HAODS
Apr 26-29	*Will Any Gentleman*	Shiplake Players
May 9-13	*Guys and Dolls*	Reading Amateur Theatrical Society
May 17-20	Kenton Drama Festival	
Jun 24	*Show Biz '72*	Henley Children's Theatre Group

Jul 19-22	*The Heiress*	HAODS
Aug 15/16	*Ballets Minerva*	Balmin Productions Ltd
Sep 21-23	*The Gondoliers*	Reading Musical Society
Oct 2	Southern Arts Association Nell Dunn, Peter Porter, EA Whitehead & Shena Mackay Talk about their writing.	
Oct 19-21	*Penny for a Song*	The Henley Players
Oct 30/Nov 4	*The Mikado*	HAODS
Dec 1-9	*The Wizard of Oz*	Caversham Park Theatre
Dec 3	*As according to Kossoff*	David Kossoff
Dec 28-30	*Puss in Boots*	Henley Children's Theatre Group

1973 — The Kenton Theatre

Jan 1-5	*Ballets Minerva*	Ballets Minerva Prod
Jan 10-13	*Toad of Toad Hall*	The Henley Players
Feb 9/10	*The Four Seasons*	Yorkshire Theatre Co
Apr 5-7	*Love by Appointment*	Shiplake Players
Apr 27/May 6	*Fiddler on the Roof*	HAODS
May 16-19	Second Kenton Drama Festival	County Drama Assoc
May 21-26	*Oklahoma!*	Woodley Light Operatic Society
Jun 2	*That's Entertainment*	Henley Children's Theatre Group
Jun 7-9	*Dark of the Moon*	The Henley Players
Jun 18-23	*When all the World is Young, Lad*	Philos Productions
Jun 25-30	*The Mollusc*	,,
Jul 2-7	*Anna Christie*	,,
Jul 18-21	*Anastasia*	HAODS
Oct 17	Fashion Show	Henley Ladies Circle and Facy's
Oct 18-20	*A Chorus of Murder*	Yorkshire Theatre Co
Oct 23-27	*The Boy Friend*	Reading Amateur Theatrical Society
Nov 1-3	*Hedda Gabler*	The Henley Players
Nov 13-17	*It's Our Pleasure*	HAODS
Dec 7/8 & Dec 14/15	*Alice in Wonderland*	Kenton Theatre Childrens Group
Dec 27-29	*Aladdin*	Henley Childrens Theatre Group

1974 — The Kenton Theatre

Jan 10-12	*The Thwarting of Baron Bolligrew*	The Henley Players
Feb 23	*Under Milk Wood*	Swansea Little Theatre
Mar 1	*Ballets Minerva*	Ballets Minerva Prod
Mar 2	*Cyril Fletcher One Man Show*	
Mar 22-23	*Kiss Me Kate*	HAODS
Apr 3	*A Fashion Spectacular*	Young Generation
Apr 26-27	*Separate Tables*	Shiplake Players
Apr 30-May 4	*Old Time Variety*	Reading Amateur Theatrical Society
Apr 6-11	*Barefoot in the Park*	Caversham Park Theatre
May 14-18	*Maid of the Mountains*	Woodley Light Operatic Society
May 22-25	*Oh, What a Lovely War*	The Henley Players
Jun 1	*The Young Idea*	Henley Children's Theatre Group
Jun 5-8	Third Kenton Drama Festival	
Jun 24-29	*A Tale of Three Brothers*	Philos Productions

Date	Production	Company
Jul 1-6	On Approval	,,
Jul 8-13	Juno and the Paycock	,,
Jul 17-20	The Secretary Bird	HAODS
Sep 25-28	The Importance of being Earnest	Tapestry Theatre Group
Oct 4/5	Hay Fever	,,
Oct 9-12	The Rivals	,,
Oct 24-26	The Rape of the Belt	The Henley Players
Nov 15-23	The Sound of Music	HAODS

1975 The Kenton Theatre

Date	Production	Company
Jan 9-11	The Sword of Galanta	The Henley Players
Mar 20-22	Woman in a Dressing Gown	Shiplake Players
Apr 12-19	Lock Up Your Daughters	HAODS
Apr 22-26	The Admirable Crichton	Reading Amateur Theatrical Society
Apr 30/May 3	Billy Liar	The Henley Players
May 30-31	Especially for You	Henley Children's Theatre Group
Jun 3-7	Fourth Kenton Drama Festival	
Jun 24-28	The Long and the Short and the Tall	HAODS
Jul 6-12	Madame Butterfly (Mon & Thu) The Marriage of Figaro (Tue & Fri) Tosca (Wed & Sat)	Kinecraft Opera
Sep 7	Sunday Evening at the Kenton Waltham St Lawrence Silver Band, Janet Bayles, Clive Tunley, Charles Walton.	
Sep 29/Oct 4	Carousel	Reading Operatic Society
Oct 14-18	Lady Be Good	Reading Amateur Theatrical Society
Oct 23-25	Black Comedy	The Henley Players
Nov 1	An Evening of Gilbert and Sullivan	Reading Amateur Operatic Society
Nov 10-15	Robert and Elizabeth	HAODS
Dec 31/Jan 1	Dick Whittington	Henley Children's Theatre Group

1976 The Kenton Theatre

Date	Production	Company
Jan 15	Cinderella	Ballets Minerva
Feb 26-28	The Visit	The Henley Players
Mar 13	Dave Morgan Band	
Mar 25-27	Showtime '76 Scout and Guide, Brownie and Cub Show	
Apr 19-24	Little Women – 7.30 nightly except Wed Once Upon a Story Time – 11.00am Sing a Memory – 7.30 Wed only	Redroofs Theatre Co
Apr 8-10	Dear Brutus	Shiplake Players
Apr 30/May 8	Sweet Charity	HAODS
May 19-22	Fifth Kenton Drama Festival	
May 29	The Super Sunshine Show	Henley Children's Theatre Group
Jun 26	Music from the Shows	Reading Operatic Society
Jun 29/Jul 2	Under Milk Wood	The Henley Players
Sep 30/Oct 2	The French Collection	HAODS
Oct 5-9	South Pacific	Reading Operatic Society
Nov 11-13	The Importance of Being Earnest	The Henley Players
Nov 30	A Evening of Magic	Home Counties Magic Society
Dec 1-4	Calamity Jane	Woodley Light Operatic Society

Dec 10/11 & 17/18	The Incredible Vanishing!!!	Caversham Park Theatre
Dec 29/Jan 1	Beauty and the Beast	Henley Children's Theatre Group

1977 — The Kenton Theatre

Jan 6-15	Where the Rainbow Ends	Redroofs Theatre Co
Jan 27	Hansel and Gretel & Sonatas	Ballets Minerva
Jan 29	Dave Morgan Jazz Band	
Feb 12	Abracadabra	Home Counties Magical Society
Feb 13	Sunday Night Concert	Jane Salmon ('cello)
Mar 4/5	Concert – Uel Decme with Hugh Stewart & David Sutton	
Mar 6	Sunday Night Concert	Albinoni Ensemble
Mar 16-19	Tom Jones	Reading Amateur Theatrical Society
Mar 24-26	Mourning Becomes Electra	The Henley Players
Apr 2	The Beggars Opera	Spectrum Theatre Group
Apr 16	Concert	Waltham St Lawrence Silver Band
Apr 21-23	Three Piece Suite, Fumed Oak, Still Life, Hands Across the Sea.	Shiplake Players
Apr 29/May 7	Hello Dolly	HAODS
May 11-14	Sixth Kenton Drama Festival	
May 17-21	Brigadoon	Woodley Light Operatic Society
May 28	The Silver Jubilation	Henley Children's Theatre Group
Jun 18	Concert	HAODS
Jun 28/Jul 1	The Hollow Crown	The Henley Players
Jul 2	The Maid Mistress and The Old Maid and the Thief	Spectrum Theatre Group
Oct 3-8	HMS Pinafore and Annie Prothero	Reading Amateur Operatic Society
Oct 18-27	Absurd Person Singular	HAODS
Oct 25-29	Dummy Run	Philos Productions
Oct 31/Nov 5	Babes in the Wood	Woodley Light Operatic Society
Nov 8-12	Jack the Ripper	Reading Amateur Operatic Society
Nov 19	I Got Gershwin	Spectrum Theatre Group
Nov 24-28	Habeas Corpus	The Henley Players
Nov 29/Dec 3	Babes in the Wood	Woodley Light Operatic Society
Dec 8-10	Jack and the Beanstalk	Caversham Park Theatre
Dec 15	Sonatas and The Wizard of Oz	Ballets Minerva
Dec 28-31	Humpty Dumpty	Henley Children's Theatre Group

1978 — The Kenton Theatre

Jan 26	Dave Morgan Jazz Band	
Mar 1-4	She Stoops to Conquer	The Henley Players
Mar 11	Olde Tyme Music Hall	Lions Club of Henley
Mar 16-18	Move Over, Mrs Markham	Shiplake Players
Mar 27/Apr 8	The Editor Regrets (World Première prior to West End opening)	
Apr 15	Pot Pourri	Spectrum Theatre Group
Apr 29/May 6	Oklahoma!	HAODS
May 9-13	White Horse Inn	Woodley Light Operatic Society

May 17-20	Seventh Kenton Drama Festival		Apr 23/May 5	*Rattle of a Simple Man*	The Henley Theatre Co David Tudor productions
May 27	*Bye-Bye Blues*	Henley Children's Theatre Group	May 7-12	*Camelot*	Woodley Light Operatic Society
Jun 10	*Salome* and *The Death of Pilate*	Spectrum Theatre Group	May 16-19	Eighth Kenton Drama Festival	
Jul 15	*A Gala Evening*	Opera Camerata	May 26	*Espana*	Maria Rosa Co
Sep 7-9	*Blue Comedy*	The Henley Players	Jun 2	*The Saturday Show*	Henley Children's Theatre Group
Sep 10	Club Night comes to the Kenton		Jun 23	*Opera Cameos*	Thames Opera
Sep 21/Oct 4	*The Lady from the Sea*	David Tudor Presents	Jun 29/30	*The Yeomen of the Guard*	Chameleon Arts
Oct 6-7	*Cosi Fan Tutte*	Chameleon Arts	Jul 1	*Olde Tyme Music Hall*	Penny Cole
Oct 17-21	*The Constant Wife*	HAODS	Jul 4	*Varsity Blue* Modern and medieval music	Oxford Colleges
Oct 30/Nov 4	*Lisbon Story*	Reading Amateur Theatrical Society	Sep 6-9	*Edwardian Soiree*	HAODS
Nov 28/Dec 3	*Hotel Paradiso*	The Henley Players	Sep 11-15	*A Midsummer Night's Dream*	The Henley Players
Dec 12-16	*Cinderella*	Spectrum Theatre Group	Sep 17-29	*Living Together*	Henley Repertory Co
Dec 27-30	*Aladdin*	Henley Children's Theatre Group	Oct 1-13	*Aurelia*	,,
			Oct 15-27	*Abigail's Party*	,,
1979	**The Kenton Theatre**		Oct 28	*Opera Cameos*	Henley Opera
Jan 13	Dave Morgan Jazz Band		Nov 6-10	*Table Manners*	HAODS
Jan 21	Roy Hudd's Music Hall		Nov 13-17	*Guys and Dolls*	Reading Amateur Theatrical Society
Feb 13	*Opus 5* and *The Snow Queen*	Ballets Minerva	Nov 28/Dec 1	*Cause Celebre*	The Henley Players
Feb 14-17	*A Sense of Occasion*	Anthony Roye	Dec 6-8	*The Squire of Topsyturvia*	Caversham Park Theatre
Feb 23-24	Dave Morgan's Jazz Band		Dec 11-15	*The Miracle Worker*	Judith Cluer
Mar 7-10	*Masks of Women* *Antigone* and *Lysistrata*	The Henley Players	**1980**	**The Kenton Theatre**	
Mar 15-17	*Suddenly at Home*	Shiplake Players	Jan 1-5	*Ruddigore*	Berkshire Youth Opera Group
Mar 19-24	*Patience*	Reading Amateur Operatic Society			
Mar 31/Apr 7	*Gigi*	HAODS			
Apr 21	*Viennese Concert*	Henley Opera Workshop			

Jan 15-19	Finian's Rainbow	Woodley Light Operatic Society
Feb 4-9	Sherlock's Last Case	Royal Touring
Mar 5-8	Flint	The Henley Players
Mar 20-22	Everything in the Garden	Shiplake Players
Mar 29	Victorian Extravaganza	Mary Hopkin, Tony Visconti
Apr 14-19	Half a Sixpence	HAODS
Apr 23-26	A Tomb with a View	Reading Amateur Operatic Society
May 3	The Marriage of Figaro	Chameleon Arts
May 13-17	Ninth Kenton Drama Festival	
May 21-24	Stevie	
May 26/Jun 7	The Prospect Behind Us	Henley Repertory Co
Jun 16-28	The Unvarnished Truth (World Première)	
Jul 1	Alan Clayson & The Argonauts and The Zoo Story	Windsor Guild
Jul 13	Razzle-Dazzle	Henley Children's Theatre Group
Sep 6	Macbeth	Independent Opera
Sep 10-13	Who's Afraid of Virginia Woolf	The Henley Players
Sep 16-27	Relatively Speaking	Bill Kenwright presents
Oct 1-4	We'll Meet Again	HAODS
Oct 16-18	The Duchess of Malfi	Royal Touring
Oct 20-25	Dirty Linen	Bill Kenwright and Alan Cluer
Nov 4-8	A Voyage Round my Father	HAODS
Nov 18-22	Lock Up Your Daughters	Reading Amateur Theatrical Society
Nov 26-29	The Wanton Wife	The Henley Players
Dec 3-6	Under Milk Wood	Judith Cluer
Dec 27/Jan 1	Puss in Boots	Henley Children's Theatre Group

1981 The Kenton Theatre

Jan 13-17	Oklahoma!	Woodley Light Operatic Society
Feb 6	Youth Talent Contest	Henley Lions Club
Feb 7	An Evening with Vince Hill and Friends	
Mar 19-21	A Letter from the General	Shiplake Players
Apr 4-11	HMS Pinafore	HAODS
Apr 14	Duncan Dragon Show	Roger Tear Productions
Apr 21-25	Hansel and Gretel	Chameleon Opera
May 12-16	Tenth Kenton Drama Festival	
May 23-30	Bedroom Farce	Judith Cluer
Jun 5-6	The Greatest Little Show in Town	Henley Children's Theatre Group
Jun 9-13	Kiss me, Kate	Woodley Light Operatic Society
Jun 20	George Chisholm and Keith Smith's Hefty Jazz	
Sep 5	Espana	Maria Rosa
Oct 2/3	Light Entertainment Evening	
Oct 23	Courtship Extracts from Jane Austin with music	
Oct 29	Peter Piper's Puppets	
Nov 17-21	The Family Dance	HAODS
Nov 25-28	What the Butler Saw	The Henley Players
Dec 3	A Funny Kind of Evening with David Kossoff	Roger Tear Productions

Date	Production	Company
Dec 10-13	*Fringe Benefits*	Shiplake Players
Dec 29/Jan 2	*Jack and the Beanstalk*	Henley Children's Theatre Group

1982 The Kenton Theatre

Date	Production	Company
Jan 9	*Salute to Broadway*	Maidenhead Musical Comedy Society
Jan 12-16	*Charlie Girl*	Woodley Light Operatic Society
Feb 20	*Salute to Broadway*	Maidenhead Musical Comedy Society
Feb 22	*The Magic Monkey Show*	
Feb 23	*Paul Doran and the Shadowstring Puppet Theatre*	
Mar 17-20	*Hay Fever*	The Henley Players
Mar 27/Apr 3	*Cowardy Custard*	HAODS
Apr 10	George Chisholm with Keith Smith and his Hefty Jazz	
Apr 17	*A Touch of Spring*	Rotary Club of Henley
Apr 26/May 1	*Stage Struck*	
May 11-15	Eleventh Kenton Drama Festival	
Jun 15-19	*My Fair Lady*	Woodley Light Operatic Society
Jul 9/10	*Wakey, Wakey*	Henley Children's Theatre Group
Jul 17-31	*It's a Small World After All*	
Aug 1	*Espana*	Maria Rosa
Oct 7-9	*Franglais '82*	HAODS
Oct 12-13	*Cider with Rosie*	Jill Freud Company
Oct 20-23	*Absent Friends*	The Henley Players
Oct 26-28	*Straight from the Heart* Olde Tyme Music Hall in Aid of Sacred Heart School	
Nov 9	*One Portion Sweet and Sour Ham – A Collection of Witty and Amusing Poems*	
Dec 7-11	*Half a Sixpence*	Woodley Light Operatic Society
Dec 15-18	*Dear Octopus*	HAODS
Dec 28/Jan 1	*Babes in the Wood*	Henley Children's Theatre Group

1983 The Kenton Theatre

Date	Production	Company
Jan 12-15	*The Adventures of a Bear called Paddington*	The Henley Players
Jan 18/19	*The Magical Voyage of Sinbad the Sailor*	Proteus Theatre Co
Mar 2-5	*The Day after the Fair*	Alan Cluer
Mar 23-26	*The Captain of Kopenick*	The Henley Players
Apr 2-9	*Joseph and the Amazing Technicolour Dreamcoat*	Judith Cluer
Apr 13	Filming for *Rhythm on Two* Tickets available to public	British Broadcasting Corporation
Apr 23-30	*Funny Girl*	HAODS
May 5-7	*How's the World Treating You?*	Shiplake Players
May 10-14	Twelfth Kenton Drama Festival	
Jun 3-4	*Summer Follies*	Henley Children's Theatre Group
Jun 14-18	*Guys and Dolls*	Woodley Light Operatic Society
Jun 20-25	*Mrs Cole's Music Hall*	
Jul 6-9	*Salad Days*	Caversham Theatre Group
Sep 7	*Salero*	Maria Rosa
Sep 27/Oct 1	*Barefoot in the Park*	The Henley Players

Oct 6-8	Mixed Doubles and Streuth	The Henley Players HAODS
Oct 15-16	Sheila Steafel	Hunter James
Oct 27-29	Olde Tyme Music Hall	Berkshire Women's Institute
Nov 29/Dec 3	Lady Windermere's Fan	HAODS
Dec 6	Hamlet 7.30pm Miracle Plays 2pm & 9.30pm	Wooden O Theatre Company
Dec 27-31	Snow White and the Seven Dwarfs	Henley Children's Theatre Group

1984 — The Kenton Theatre

Jan 4-7	The Silver Sword and Down in the Valley	Berkshire Youth Opera
Jan 17-21	Hello Dolly (Recorded by the BBC Radio 4 for broadcasting in Feb or Mar)	Woodley Light Operatic Society
Jan 27	Concert	Anthony Hopkins (Musician and Composer)
Feb 23-25	The Time is Ripe – A Musical Evening	St John's Ambulance Cadet Division
Mar 17	The Reading Barbarettes	
Mar 28-31	The Threepenny Opera	The Henley Players
Apr 23-28	Cabaret	HAODS
May 16-19	Thirteenth Kenton Drama Festival	
Jul 6 & 7	Music Box	Henley Children's Theatre Group
Jun 12-16	Fiddler on the Roof	Woodley Light Operatic Society
Jul 30/ Aug 6 & 13	Three Play Readings	HAODS
Sep 21	Talent Contest	Royal National Lifeboat Institution
Sep 26-29	The Importance of Being Earnest	The Henley Players
Oct 1-6	John Doe Day	
Nov 20-24	The Prime of Miss Jean Brodie	HAODS
Dec 11 & 12	Pickwick Papers	Jill Freud & Co
Dec 20-29	Dick Whittington	HAODS

1985 — The Kenton Theatre

Jan 1-5	Who Killed Santa Claus?	The Henley Players
Jan 7-12	Pinoccho	Generation Theatre Co
Jan 15-19	South Pacific	Woodley Light Operatic Society
Apr 12-20	Guys and Dolls	HAODS
May 1-4	Macbeth	The Henley Players
May 14-18	Fourteenth Kenton Drama Festival	
May 28	The Great Soprendo's Monster Magical Show	
Jun 17-22	HMS Pinafore	Woodley Light Operatic Society
Jun 24-29	The Two of Us	Initial Productions (Theatre) Ltd
Aug 2	Cluedo	Who dunnit We dunnit!
Sep 18-21	Music Hall	HAODS
Oct 2-5	A Flea in her Ear	The Henley Players
Oct 18	London Harpsichord Ensemble	Henley Concerts
Nov 2	House of Spirit Transfiguration and Clairvoyance	Lee Everett and Bill Landis
Nov 19-23	An Inspector Calls	HAODS
Nov 25	Youth Speaks	Henley Rotary Club

Nov 29	Ian Partridge	Henley Concerts
Dec 4-7	Our Town	Judith Cluer
Dec 11-14	Enemies	King James' College
Dec 30/Jan 4	Cinderella	Henley Children's Theatre Group

1986   The Kenton Theatre

Jan 13-18	Hans Andersen	Woodley Light Operatic Society
Jan 19	Opera Gems	Chameleon Opera
Jan 31	Mortimer's Miscellany	
Mar 7	James Gibb (Piano)	Henley Concerts
Apr 11-19	Carousel	HAODS
Apr 30/May 3	The Caucasian Chalk Circle	The Henley Players
May 13-17	Fifteenth Kenton Drama Festival	
Jun 7	Don't Shoot Me, I'm Only the Piano Player	David Scheel
Jun 9-14	Calamity Jane	Woodley Light Operatic Society
Jun 28	Dixieland Jazz	
Sep 10-13	Fanny Kemble at Home	Peter Wilson presents
Oct 17-25	Fiddler on the Roof	HAODS
Nov 11-15	The Dresser	Judith Cluer presents
Nov 22-29	Oliver!	Masquer-aid
Dec 5	The Allegri String Quartet	Henley Concerts

1987   The Kenton Theatre

Jan 1-3	Thank you, Henley and Goodbye 1986	The Henley Players
Jan 13-17	Sugar	Woodley Light Operatic Society
Jan 23	Julian Evans (Piano)	Henley Concerts
Feb 7-8	Salute to Broadway	Generation Theatre
Mar 5-7	Youth Showcase	Henley Link Theatre
Mar 13	Uroboros Ensemble	Henley Concerts
Mar 18-21	Outside Edge	The Henley Players
Apr 3-11	How to Succeed in Business without really Trying	HAODS
May 12-16	Sixteenth Kenton Drama Festival	
May 20-30	The Norman Conquests	Judith Cluer
May 20-23	Table Manners	
May 27-30	Round and Round the Garden	
Jun 9-13	The Mikado	Woodley Light Operatic Society
Sep 14-15	The Portrait of Dorian Grey	Pictures in Focus Productions
Sep 18	A Father's Heart – Free!	Geoffrey Stevenson
Sep 30/Oct 3	Miranda	HAODS
Oct 10	An Evening with John Mortimer	
Oct 21-24	The Killing of Sister George	The Henley Players
Nov 12-21	West Side Story	HAODS
Nov 24-28	Kismet	Woodley Light Operatic Society
Dec 4	Yeoh Ean Mei (Piano)	Henley Concerts
Dec 28/Jan 2	Aladdin	Henley Children's Theatre Group

1988   The Kenton Theatre

Feb 17-20	California Suite	The Henley Players
Mar 10-19	Bernard Trapp's Unfinished Musical	
Apr 22-30	My Fair Lady	HAODS
May 10-14	Seventeenth Kenton Drama Festival	

May 18-21	*A Midsummer Night's Dream* and *The Tempest*	Henley College Theatre Group
Jun 7-11	*The Fire Raisers*	The Henley Players
Jul 16	*A Summer in the South*	Save the Regal Fund
Oct 4	Charity Special In Aid of Save the Children Fund	
Oct 19-22	*The Browning Version* and *Harlequinade*	The Henley Players
Nov 8-12	*Separate Tables*	HAODS
Nov 18-26	*Godspell*	KT Productions
Dec 2	Graham Jackson (Piano)	Henley Concerts
Dec 6-10	*The Wizard of Oz*	Woodley Light Operatic Society

1989 The Kenton Theatre

Jan 20-26	*A Fish called Wanda*	Cinema
Jan 27	The Greenwich Ensemble	Henley Concerts
Feb 1-2	*A Handful of Dust*	Cinema
Feb 3	*Willow*	,,
Feb 10-11	*Willow*	,,
Feb 22-25	*A Night with George Bernard Shaw*	The Henley Players
Feb 26	*High Spirits*	Cinema
Mar 3-10	*Dead Ringers*	,,
Mar 10	Roderick Swanston Lecturing on Haydn	Henley Concerts
Mar 20-25	*Amadeus*	Judith Cluer
Mar 31	Midnight Matinee Charity Showing *The Dressmaker*	Cinema
Apr 14 22	*Mame*	HAODS
May 3-6	*Children in Uniform*	The Henley Players
May 9	Youth Speaks Final of Public Speaking Contest	The Rotary Club
May 10-13	*The Last Emperor*	Cinema
May 16-20	Eighteenth Kenton Drama Festival	
May 26-31	*Who Framed Roger Rabbit*	Cinema
Jun 2	Old Time Music Hall	
Jun 16-23	*Charlie Chaplin – The Musical*	Cinema
Jul 9-13	*Rainman*	,,
Jul 14-20	*Dangerous Liaisons*	,,
Jul 24-29	*Gorillas in the Mist*	,,
Jul 24, 27	*Dumbo, Winnie the Pooh and Tigger too*	,,
Sep 12	*The Lonely Passion of Judith Hearne*	,,
Sep 15	*Batman*	,,
Oct 13	Bernard Roberts (Piano)	Henley Concerts
Oct 25-28	*Noises Off*	The Henley Players
Oct 30	*Indiana Jones and the Last Crusade*	Cinema
Nov 2	The London Chinese Ensemble	Henley Concerts
Nov 14-18	*The Chalk Garden*	HAODS
Nov 29/Dec 2	*The Pirates of Penzance*	Woodley Light Operatic Society
Dec 9-16	*Scrooge*	KT Productions
Dec 19-22	*The Measures Taken* and *The Exception and the Rule*	Henley College Theatre Group
Dec 27-30	*The Bear*	Cinema

1990 The Kenton Theatre

Jan 5/6	*Peter Pan – A pantomime*	Starmaker Theatre Co
Jan 18-20	*Snow White and the Seven Dwarfs*	Henley Children's Theatre Group

Jan 27	An Evening of Victorian Music, Comedy and Drama	HAODS
Feb 2	The Albion Ensemble	Henley Concerts
Feb 16-17	*Shirley Valentine*	Cinema
Feb 21-24	*Snoopy – The Musical*	Starmaker Theatre Co
Feb 26-28	*The Marriage of Figaro*	Pan Optic Theatre Co
Mar 14-17	*A Three Course Feast*	The Henley Players
Mar 23	The Medici String Quartet	Henley Concerts
Mar 26-31	*Little Shop of Horrors*	KT Productions
Apr 1-7	*New Works*	Henley College Theatre Group
Apr 20-28	*Camelot*	HAODS
May 1-5	*Ruddigore*	Crowthorne Musical Players
May 8-10	*Henry V*	Cinema
May 11/12	*The War of the Roses*	,,
May 15-19	Nineteenth Kenton Drama Festival	
May 20/21	*The Hunt for Red October*	Cinema
May 22-26	*A Dream Play*	Henley College Theatre Group
May 29/30	*Driving Miss Daisy*	Cinema
Jun 5-9	*Annie get your Gun*	Woodley Light Operatic Society
Jun 15/16	*Annie's Got a Gun*	Henley Children's Theatre Group
Jun 18-23	*Look Who's Talking*	Cinema
Jun 25/26	*Glory*	,,
Jun 27	*Dead Poet's Society*	,,
Jun 29/30	*Showcase*	Henley Musical TheatreSchool
Jul 8-12	*Driving Miss Daisy*	Cinema
Jul 13	*New York Stories*	,,
Jul 17-19	*The Phantom of the Opera*	,,
Sep 21	*Venus Peter*	,,
Sep 29/Oct 6	*The King and I*	HAODS and The Henley Musical Theatre School
Oct 9	*Pretty Woman*	Cinema
Oct 10-11	*Cinema Paradiso*	,,
Oct 12	Amanda Hurton (Piano)	Henley Concerts
Oct 14	*The Fairy Liquid Show or Paradise Retained*	
Oct 15-20	*Memphis Belle*	Cinema
Nov 21-24	*Candleford*	The Henley Players
Nov 27/Dec 3	*Iolanthe*	Woodley Light Operatic Society
Dec 14-17	*Frankenstein, the Panto*	KT Productions
Dec 28/Jan 5	*The Little Mermaid*	Cinema

1991 The Kenton Theatre

Jan 4-5	*Ghost* – 6.30 & 8.30 *The Little Mermaid* – 2.30	Cinema
Jan 9-12	*Broadway to Piccadilly* – A Revue	Starmaker
Jan 16-19	*Dick Whittington* – A Pantomime	Henley Children's Theatre Group
Jan 20	*Jazzabelles*	Henley Concerts
Jan 22-24	*Don Giovanni*	Cinema
Jan 25-29	*Home Alone*	,,
Feb 1-2	*Bird on a Wire*	,,
Feb 10	Alexander Taylor (Piano) and Robert Szente (Violin)	Henley Concerts

Feb 15-20	*Arachnaphobia*	Cinema
Feb 22	*Allegri String Quartet*	Henley Concerts
Feb 23	*Ghosts*	Cinema
Feb 26-28	*Havana*	,,
Mar 1-5	*The Sheltering Sky*	,,
Mar 8-13	*Cyrano de Bergerac*	,,
Mar 22-27	*Postcards from the Edge*	,,
Apr 12-20	*The Mikado*	HAODS
Apr 26/Mar 1	*Green Card*	Cinema
Apr 28	The Brian Haddock Big Band with The Anthony England Trio	
May 5	An Evening of Music	Anthony England and Friends
May 14-18	Twentieth Kenton Drama Festival	
May 26/Jun 1	*Regatta Day*	KT Productions
Jun 4-8	*South Pacific*	Woodley Light Operatic Society
Jun 14/15	*Me and My Ron*	Henley Children's Theatre Group
Jun 26-29	*Born in the Gardens*	The Henley Players
Jun 30	Sunday Night Live Rock & Pop Nite	
Jul 7	Waltham St Lawrence Silver Band	
Jul 8-11	*Dances with Wolves*	Cinema
Jul 12-18	*Sleeping with the Enemy*	,,
Jul 19-24	*Hamlet*	,,
Sep 6-12	*Silence of the Lambs*	,,
Sep 13-18	*Fantasia*	,,
Sep 23-26	*Robin Hood Prince of Thieves*	,,
Sep 27/Oct 2	*Truly, Madly, Deeply*	,,
Oct 4	Caroline Dale ('cello) and Sally Heath (Piano)	Henley Concerts
Oct 14-19	*Stepping Out*	HAODS
Oct 25-30	*Meeting Venus*	Cinema
Nov 11-16	*A Man for all Seasons*	HAODS
Nov 23-30	*The Secret Diary of Adrian Mole Aged 13¾*	KT Productions
Dec 1	Henley Concerts	
Dec 4-7	*Once upon a Time*	Starmaker
Dec 13-18	*Dead Again*	Cinema
Dec 31/Jan 4	*Puss in Boots*	Henley Children's Theatre Group
1992	**The Kenton Theatre**	
Jan 6-11	*The Fisher King*	Cinema
Jan 14-18	*The Boy Friend*	Woodley Light Operatic Society
Jan 20	Youth Speaks Contest	Rotary Club of Henley
Jan 21-23	*The Commitments*	Cinema
Jan 24-31	*The Addams Family*	,,
Feb 7-14	*Prospero's Books*	,,
Feb 17-20	*Hot Shots*	,,
Feb 21-26	*Blame it on the Bellboy*	,,
Feb 27	Sarah Ewins (Violin) and Yoshiko Endo (Piano)	Henley Concerts
Feb 29	Mungo Jerry in Concert	KT Productions
Mar 8-13	*Frankie and Johnny*	Cinema
Mar 20	The Holywell Ensemble	Henley Concerts
Mar 28/ Apr 4	*Spider's Web*	KT Productions
Apr 6-9	*Barton Fink*	Cinema
Apr 24/May 2	*Hello, Dolly*	HAODS
May 4-9	*Fried Green Tomatoes at the Whistlestop Cafe*	Cinema

May 12-16	Twenty-first Kenton Drama Festival	
May 18-21	*JFK*	Cinema
May 25-27	*Father of the Bride*	,,
May 28-30	*Hear My Song*	,,
Jun 9-15	*Kiss Me, Kate*	Woodley Light Operatic Society
Jun 19/20	*Double Whammy*	Henley Children's Theatre Group
Jun 24-27	*Once Upon a Time*	Starmaker
Jul 22	The London and Continental School Of Dance and The North Carolina School of the Arts	KT Productions
Sep 11-16	*Howard's End*	Cinema
Sep 18/19	*The Long Day Closes*	,,
Sep 24-26	*Here's a How-de-Doo*	Valley Productions
Oct 6-10	*Night Must Fall*	The Henley Players
Oct 11	Jeremy Menuhin (Piano)	Henley Concerts
Oct 20-24	*Lettice and Lovage*	HAODS
Oct 28-30	Old Time Music Hall	Women's Institute
Nov 1	Gerald Garcia (Piano) and Clive Conway (Flute)	Henley Concerts
Nov 4-6	*Holiday for Simon*	AJS Productions
Nov 13-21	*Annie*	HAODS
Nov 24-28	*Ruddigore*	Woodley Light Operatic Society
Dec 9-19	*Aladdin*	KT Productions
Dec 29/Jan 2	*Cinderella*	Henley Children's Theatre Group

1993   The Kenton Theatre

Jan 8-13	*Howard's End*	Cinema
Jan 24	Nicola and Alexandra Bibby	Henley Concerts
Jan 27	Youth Speaks	Rotary Club of Henley
Jan 29 Feb 3	*Sister Act*	Cinema
Feb 5-10	*Peter's Friends*	,,
Feb 12-17	*Home Alone 2*	,,
Feb 19-24	*Blade Runner*	,,
Feb 24	Half-Term Holiday Show 11.00am & 2.30	
Feb 20-26	*Beauty and the Beast* – 5.30	,,
Feb 26	*Bodyguard* – 7.45	,,
Mar 8	Young Musician Competition	Rotary Club of Henley
Mar 12-17	*A Few Good Men*	Cinema
Mar 19	The Lyric String Quartet	Henley Concerts
Mar 31/Apr 3	*A Small Family Business*	The Henley Players
Apr 16-24	*The Pajama Game*	Henley Amateur Operatic
Apr 26/May 1	*Chaplin*	Cinema
May 6-8	The Ministry Jesus, the Man and his Miracles	One Solitary Life Players
May 11-15	Twenty-second Kenton Drama Festival	
May 21-29	*Cabaret*	KT Productions
Jun 4-12	*Anything Goes*	Woodley Light Operatic Society
Jun 17	Rabbi Lionel Blue	
Jun 25/26	*From Rubbish with Love*	Henley Children's Theatre Group
Jul 5-11	*Sommersby*	Cinema
Jul 12-17	*Indecent Proposal*	Cinema
Sep 10	*Three Men in a Boat*	KT Productions
Sep 11	Grand Charity Show	
Sep 13-18	*Made in America*	Cinema

Sep 22-25	The Beggars Opera	Valley Productions
Sep 27/Oct 2	Orlando	Cinema
Oct 4-9	In the Line of Fire	,,
Oct 11-16	The Firm	,,
Oct 26-30	Steel Magnolias	The Henley Players
Nov 1-5	Much Ado About Nothing	Cinema
Nov 22-27	The Fugitive	,,
Nov 15-20	A Chorus of Disapproval	HAODS
Dec 8-18	Oliver!	KT Productions
Dec 19, 23, 24	Joe Brown and the Bruvvers	
Dec 28/Jan 1	Mother Goose	Henley Children's Theatre Group

1994 The Kenton Theatre

Jan 3-8	The Secret Garden	Cinema
Jan 11-15	Bless the Bride	Woodley Light Operatic Society
Jan 18-22	Rock Nativity	Starmaker Theatre Co
Jan 24-26	Tina – "What's love got to do with it?"	Cinema
Jan 26	Youth Speaks	Rotary Club of Henley
Jan 27	Sleepless in Seattle	Cinema
Feb 5-12	The Wizard of Oz	Henley Musical Theatre School
Feb 14-17	Jurassic Park	Cinema
Feb 19	Young Musicians	Henley Rotary Club
Feb 20	The Marwood Family Ensemble	Henley Concerts
Feb 21-25	The Piano	Cinema
Feb 26	Comedy at the Kenton	Bound and Gagged Comedy Club
Feb 28/Mar 2	A Perfect World	Cinema
Mar 3	A Funny kind of Evening with David Kossof	
Mar 5	Comedy at the Kenton	Bound and Gagged Comedy Club
Mar 7	Youth Speaks District Semi-Finals	Rotary Club of Henley
Mar 8/9	Les Enfants du Paradis	Cinema
Mar 10/11	Much Ado about Nothing	Cinema
Mar 12	Comedy at the Kenton	Bound and Gagged Comedy Club
Mar 22-26	Waiting in the Wings	The Henley Players
Mar 27	The Haffner Wind Ensemble	Henley Concerts
Apr 15-23	Guys and Dolls	HAODS
Apr 25-30	Mrs Doubtfire	Cinema
May 5	A Funny kind of Evening with David Kossof	
May 7	A British Country Music Concert	Nettlebed Country Music Club
May 10-14	Twenty-third Kenton Drama Festival	
May 25/Jun 4	Showboat	KT Productions
Jun 10	Steafel Solo	KT Productions
Jun 14-18	Oklahoma!	Woodley Light Operatic Society
Jun 23-25	Frideswide	One Solitary Life Players
Jun 28/Jul 1	Three Men in a Boat	KT Productions
Jul 5/6	Turn Your Radio On	Henley Children's Theatre Group
Jul 11-16	Four Weddings and a Funeral	Cinema
Jul 18-21	Schindler's List	,,
Jul 22-23	Shadowlands	,,
Sep 12-15	Four Weddings and a Funeral	,,

Sep 15	The Mask	,,
Sep 16-17	Wyatt Earp	,,
Oct 3-4	Little Buddha	,,
Oct 6-8	The Remains of the Day	,,
Oct 14	The Vanburgh Quartet	Henley Concerts
Oct 25-29	An Inspector Calls	The Henley Players
Oct 31/Nov 5	Speed	Cinema
Nov 18-26	Chicago	HAODS
Nov 28/Dec 3	Forrest Gump	Cinema
Dec 6-10	The Yeomen of the Guard	Woodley Light Operatic Society
Dec 12-15	Shadowlands	Cinema
Dec 16-18	Joe Brown and the Bruvvers	Joe Brown Productions

1995 The Kenton Theatre

Jan 6-7	Jack and the Beanstalk	Henley Children's Theatre Group
Jan 19-28	Robinson Crusoe	KT Productions
Jan 30	Youth Speaks Competition	Rotary Club of Henley-on-Thames
Jan 31/Feb 4	Miracle on 34th Street	Cinema
Feb 13-18	When We are Married	HAODS
Feb 20-23	The Lion King	Cinema
Feb 24-25	Four Weddings and a Funeral	,,
Mar 3-4	Only You	,,
Mar 11	Marian Montgomery	
Mar 13-14	The Nutcracker	New York City Ballet
Mar 15-17	Camilla	Cinema
Mar 18-25	Henley Youth Festival	
Apr 7-22	Barnum	HAODS
May 9-13	Twenty-fourth Kenton Drama Festival	
May 2-6	Behold Your King	One Solitary Life Players
May 20-27	Wind in the Willows	KT Productions
May 29/Jun 3	The Madness of King George	Cinema
Jun 9	Born to Perform	
Jun 13-17	My Fair Lady	Woodley Light Operatic Society
Jun 27/Jul 1	Tonight at 8.30	The Henley Players
Jul 3-7	The Madness of King George	Cinema
Jul 8	A Country Music Concert	
Jul 10-15	Circle of Friends	Cinema
Jul 16	Spectrum and Friends in Concert	
Sep 8-14	Waterworld	Cinema
Sep 16	An Evening of Edwardian Music Hall	
Sep 25-30	The Merchant of Venice	HAODS
Oct 5-7	Daisy Pulls it Off	Starmaker Theatre Co
Oct 12-14	Zigger-Zagger	,,
Oct 24-28	Arsenic and Old Lace	The Henley Players
Nov 3-11	Nunsense	KT Productions
Nov 17-25	Jack the Ripper	HAODS
Nov 28/Dec 2	The King and I	Masquerade Theatre Company
Dec 4-9	Carousel	Woodley Light Operatic Society
Dec 10, 16, and 17	Joe Brown and the Bruvvers	
Dec 21-23	Christmas Crackers	KT Productions

1996	The Kenton Theatre	
Jan 1-6	*Aladdin*	Henley Children's Theatre Group
Jan 8-13	*A Walk in the Clouds*	Cinema
Jan 15-20	*Apollo 13*	,,
Jan 22-27	*Goldeneye*	,,
Jan 29	Youth Speaks Competition	Rotary Club of Henley-on-Thames
Jan 30/Feb 3	*The Bridges of Madison County*	Cinema
Feb 4	*All That Jazz*	Monica Cleaver
Feb 12-17	*French Kiss*	Cinema
Feb 26	*Plaza Suite*	HAODS
Mar 4-9	*Crimson Tide*	Cinema
Mar 10-16	Henley Youth Festival	
Mar 26-30	*Peril at End House*	The Henley Players
Apr 1-6	*A Little Princess*	
Apr 19-27	*South Pacific*	HAODS
Apr 30/May 4	*High Society*	Masquerade Theatre Company
May 6-8	*Braveheart*	Cinema
May 9-11	*Babe*	,,
May 13-18	Twenty-fifth Kenton Drama Festival	
May 24/Jun 8	*42nd Street*	KT Productions
Jun 11-15	*The Pajama Game*	Woodley Light Operatic Society
Jun 16	*Annie's on the Run*	Henley Children's Theatre Group
Jun 18-22	*Sense and Sensibility*	Cinema
Jun 24-26	*Get Shorty*	,,
Jun 27-29	*In the Bleak Midwinter*	,,
Jul 1	Kazak Cultural Evening	Equip Trust
Jul 8-10	*Dangerous Minds*	Cinema
Jul 11-13	*Richard III*	,,
Sep 2-7	*Twister*	,,
Sep 13-21	*The Boy Friend*	HAODS
Sep 23-28	*Independence day*	Cinema
Oct 7-12	*Sweet Charity*	Masquerade Theatre Company
Oct 22-26	*Dancing at Lughnasa*	The Henley Players
Nov 5-9	*Bugsy Malone*	Henley Musical Theatre School
Nov 11-16	*Emma*	Cinema
Nov 24-30	*Gaslight*	HAODS
Dec 3-7	*Gigi*	Woodley Light Operatic Society
Dec 14-15	Joe Brown and his Bruvvers	
Dec 20-28	*Dick Whittington and his Cat*	KT Productions
Dec 31/Jan 4	*Babes in the Wood*	Henley Children's Theatre School

1997	The Kenton Theatre	
Jan 6-7	*Michael Collins*	Cinema
Jan 8-11	*Twelfth Night*	,,
Jan 20	Youth Speaks	Rotary Club of Henley-on-Thames
Jan 21-25	*Brassed Off*	Cinema
Jan 25	*The Care Bears Magical Story Book* 11.30 & 2.30	KT Productions with Royston Productions
Jan 27/Feb 1	*Romeo and Juliet*	Actors Bold
Feb 11-15	*Ring Round the Moon*	The Henley Players
Feb 17-22	*Jude*	Cinema
Feb 20	*Secrets of your Life*	Richard Dawkins

Feb 21	The Half Term Holiday Show 11.30 & 2.30	Mister Chris and Martin Monkey
Mar 3-5	*Stepping Out*	Masquerade Musical Theatre Company
Mar 10-15	*The Henley Youth Festival*	
Mar 16	*A Chance to Dance*	Harlequin School of Dancing
Mar 21-22	*Dance if it Makes You Happy*	Linda Sweetzer School
Apr 3-12	*La Cage aux Folles*	HAODS
Apr 23-26	*The Promise*	One Solitary Life Players
Apr 27	Young Musician	Rotary Club of Henley-on-Thames
Apr 28-30	*Othello*	Cinema
May 1-3	*Fierce Creatures*	,,
May 6-10	Twenty-sixth Kenton Drama Festival	
May 12-15	*A Portrait of a Lady*	Cinema
May 16-17	*True Blue*	,,
May 19-22	*In Love and War*	,,
May 23-24	*Flirting with Disaster*	,,
May 26-29	*Ransom*	,,
May 30-31	*Secrets and Lies*	,,
Jun 2-3	*The Curse of the Basketcases* and *A Music Hall Revue*	Henley Children's Theatre Group
Jun 4	*Magpie Lane*	Top Folk Band
Jun 5	*How to be a Millionaire*	Bernice Cohen
Jun 10-14	*HMS Pinafore*	Woodley Light Operatic Society
Jul 8-9 & 11-12	*La Boheme*	Camberwell Pocket Opera
Jul 10	*Music for a Summer Evening*	Ian and Jennifer Partridge
Jul 13-14	*The Buck and Bunnies Roadshow*	Graham Buck
Sep 29	*Alphabetical Order*	HAODS
Oct 14-18	*Les Liaisons Dangereuses*	The Henley Players
Oct 21-25	*An Old Time Music Hall*	Masquerade Musical Theatre Company
Oct 27/Nov 1	*The Leading Man*	Cinema
Nov 13-22	*Anything Goes*	HAODS
Nov 23	*A Melody Scrapbook 1917-1939*	
Nov 24-25	*Photographing Fairies*	Cinema
Nov 26-29	*Jane Eyre*	,,
Dec 2-6	*Hello Dolly*	Woodley Light Operatic Society
Dec 8-9	*Smillas feeling for Snow*	Cinema
Dec 10-13	*GI Jane*	,,
Dec 15-18	*Doctor Zhivago*	,,
Dec 19-21	Joe Brown and his Bruvvers	
Dec 30/Jan 2	*Dick Whittington*	Henley Children's Theatre group

1998 — The Kenton Theatre

Jan 5-19	*Welcome to Sarajevo*	Cinema
Jan 16-17	*Temptress Moon*	,,
Jan 18	*An Evening of Dance*	Harlequin School of Dance
Jan 9-15	*It's a Wonderful Life*	Cinema
Jan 19-24	*Alien Resurrection*	,,
Jan 26	*Youth Speaks*	Rotary Club of Henley-on-Thames
Jan 29-31	*Paradise Road*	Cinema
Feb 2-4	*Looking for Richard*	,,
Feb 5-7	*The Full Monty*	,,
Feb 9-10	*Hamlet*	,,

Feb 11-12	Heat and Dust	Cinema
Feb 13-14	Keep the Aspidistra Flying	,,
Feb 16-17	La Huitieme Jour	,,
Feb 18-19	Regeneration	,,
Feb 20-21	Mrs Brown	,,
Feb 24-28	A Murder is Announced	Masquerade Theatre Company
Mar 2-7	The Henley Youth Festival	
Mar 17-21	The Deep Blue Sea	The Henley Players
Mar 22	The Schubert Ensemble of London	Henley Festival Friends
Mar 24-26	The Full Monty	Cinema
Mar 27-28	The Wings of the Dove	,,
Apr 8-18	Me and My Girl	HAODS
Apr 20-21	Wilde	Cinema
Apr 22-23	Amistad	,,
Apr 24-25	Evita	,,
May 1-2	The (ever so slightly Jazzy) Piano Concert	Anthony England presents
May 5-9	Twenty-seventh Kenton Drama Festival	
May 18-23	The Hot Mikado	KT Productions
May 26-27	Ulee's Gold	Cinema
May 28-30	Titanic	,,
Jun 2-6	Godspell	Starmaker Theatre Company
Jun 9-13	Cabaret	Woodley Light Operatic Society
Jun 20-27	Blue Remembered Hills	HAODS
Jul 7-11	Cosi fan Tutte	Camberwell Pocket Opera
Jul 17-18	Lights, Camera, Dance	Harlequin School of Dance
Oct 13-17	The Lady's Not for Burning	The Henley Players
Oct 20-24	Abigail's Party	Masquerade Theatre Company
Oct 26-28	The Land Girls	Cinema
Oct 29-31	The Gingerbread Man	,,
Nov 6-14	Oh! What a Lovely War	HAODS
Nov 24-26	The Wiz	Henley Musical Theatre School
Nov 30/Dec 2	The Spanish Prisoner	Cinema
Dec 3-5	Red Corner	,,
Dec 8-12	The Mikado	Woodley Light Operatic Society
Dec 14-15	La Boheme	Cinema
Dec 16-18	Grease	,,
Dec 19-20	Joe Brown and his Bruvvers	
Dec 29/Jan 2	Snow White and the Seven Dwarfs	Henley Children's Theatre Group

1999 The Kenton Theatre

Jan 8, 9, 15, 16, 22, 23	Cinderella	KT Productions
Jan 11-13	The Adventures of Robin Hood	Cinema
Jan 18-20	Great Expectations	,,
Jan 24	Harlequin School of Dance	
Jan 25	Youth Speaks	Henley Rotary Club
Jan 27-28	Hope Floats	Cinema
Jan 29-30	The Exorcist	,,
Feb 4-6	Dancing at Lughnasa	,,
Feb 8-10	Victory	,,

Feb 12-13	Momentz	,,
Feb 23-24	The Last Days of Disco	,,
Feb 25-27	The Governess	,,
Mar 9-13	Arms and the Man	The Henley Players
Mar 14-20	Henley Youth Festival	
Mar 22, 23, 25	Hilary and Jackie	Cinema
Mar 24, 26, 28	What Dreams may Come	,,
Mar 25-27	Rush Hour	,,
Apr 10-17	Carousel	HAODS
Apr 19, 20, 22	Elizabeth	Cinema
Apr 21, 23, 24	Little Voice	,,
Apr 22-24	Saving Private Ryan	,,
Apr 25	Friendly Opera	HAODS
May 4-8	Twenty-eighth Kenton Drama Festival	
May 17-22	What the Butler Saw	KT Productions
May 24, 27, 28	The Mask of Zorro	Cinema
May 25, 27	You've got Mail	,,
May 26, 28	Shakespeare in Love	,,
Jun 8-12	Guys and Dolls	Woodley Light Operatic Society
Jul 15-16	You make me feel like Dancing	Harlequin School of Dance
Oct 12-16	Blithe Spirit	The Henley Players
Oct 22-23	Be Our Guest	Henley Musical Theatre School
Oct 26-28	Rushmore and Entrapment	Cinema
Oct 27-29	The Italian Job	,,
Oct 29-30	The Honest Courtesan	,,
Oct 30	The New Care Bears Magic Show	
Nov 1, 4	The Theory of Flight	Cinema
Nov 2	Touch of Evil	,,
Nov 3, 4, 5	Yellow Submarine	,,
Nov 5	Black cat, White cat	,,
Nov 12-20	Pippin	HAODS
Dec 1-4	The Journey	One Solitary Life Christian Theatre Company
Dec 7-12	Iolanthe	Woodley Light Operatic Society
Dec 15-18	Puss in Boots	Henley Children's Theatre Group
Dec 26/Jan 2	Sinbad	KT Productions

2000 — The Kenton Theatre

Jan 6-8	Shakespeare in Love	Cinema
Jan 10-12	The General's Daughter	,,
Jan 15	Step on	EJ Productions
Jan 17-19	The Clandestine Marriage	Cinema
Jan 20-22	Ride with the Devil	,,
Jan 23	An Evening of Dance	Harlequin School of Dance
Jan 24	Youth Speaks	Henley Rotary Club
Jan 26-28	The Thomas Crown Affair	Cinema
Jan 31/Feb 2	The Deep Blue Sea	,,
Feb 3-5	Bowfinger	,,
Feb 14-19	A Little Hotel on the Side	HAODS
Feb 21-23	East is East	Cinema
Feb 23	The Haunted Castle Show	

Feb 24-26	*Notting Hill*	Cinema
Feb 29/Mar 4	*Half a Sixpence*	Masquerade Musical Theatre Company
Mar 6-8	*The Titchborne Claimant*	Cinema
Mar 9-11	*Unknown Film*	,,
Mar 20-25	*Cavalcade*	The Henley Players
Mar 28	*Friendly Opera Two*	HAODS
Apr 7-15	*Orpheus in the Underworld*	HAODS
Apr 17-22	*Topsy Turvy*	Cinema
May 2-6	Twenty-ninth Kenton Drama Festival	
May 12-20	*Mack and Mabel*	KT Productions
May 22-24	*The Cider House Rules*	Cinema
May 25-27	*American Beauty*	,,
Jun 1-3	*James and the Giant Peach*	Organised Chaos Theatre Association
Jun 6-10	*Fiddler on the Roof*	Woodley Light Operatic Society
Jun 13-17	*A Millennium Variety Show*	Behind U Productions
Jun 27	*A Summer Review*	Henley Children's Theatre Group
Jul 7-8	*The Marriage of Figaro*	Candlelight Opera
Jul 21-22	*Dance Mania*	Harlequin School of Dance
Sep 18-22	*Come back to the Five and Dime Jimmy Dean, Jimmy Dean*	HAODS
Sep 25	*Lillian Bouette, Thomas L'Etienne and their Music Friends*	
Sep 26-27	*Snow falling on Cedars*	Cinema
Sep 28-30	*Gladiator*	,,
Oct 10-14	*Wild Goose Chase*	The Henley Players
Oct 17-18	*Saving Grace*	Cinema
Oct 19-21	*The Patriot*	,,
Oct 23-24	*Ballet Imaginaire*	
Nov 6-11	*Man of La Mancha*	HAODS
Nov 20-25	*Absurd Person Singular*	KT Productions
Nov 26	*A Tribute to Pat Port*	
Nov 27-29	*Sweet and Lowdown*	Cinema
Nov 30/Dec 2	*Shanghai Noon*	,,
Dec 5-9	*The Pirates of Penzance*	Woodley Light Operatic Society
Dec 11-12	*The Green Mile*	Cinema
Dec 13-15	*The Best Man*	,,
Dec 16-17	*A Showbusiness Lifetime*	Joe Brown and the Bruvvers
Dec 18-20	*Return to Me*	Cinema
Dec 21-23	*Dancer in the Dark*	,,

2001   The Kenton Theatre

Jan 1, 2, 5, 6	*Mother Goose*	Henley Children's Theatre Group
Jan 13	*Step On II*	EJ Productions
Jan 15	*Youth Speaks*	Henley Rotary Club
Jan 16-17	*The House of Mirth*	Cinema
Jan 18-20	*Titus*	,,
Jan 23-27	*Puss in Boots*	Behind U Productions
Jan 28/Feb 3	*Damn Yankees*	Masquerade Musical Theatre
Feb 4-17	*Peter Pan*	Henley Musical Theatre
Feb 19-21	*Small Time Crooks*	Cinema
Feb 22-24	*The Golden Bowl*	,,
Feb 25	*An Evening of Dance*	Harlequin School of Dance

Date	Event	Company
Feb 26/Mar 1	An Audience with Paul Daniels	
Mar 3	Stealing the Limelight	Limelight Dance Company
Mar 4	The Girl on the Bridge	Henley Film Society Cinema
Mar 5-7	Nasty Neighbours	
Mar 8-10	The Claim	,,
Mar 20-24	Last Tango in Whitby	The Henley Players
Mar 25-31	The Henley Youth Festival	
Apr 1	Bringing Out the Dead	Henley Film Society Cinema
Apr 2-4	Almost Famous	
Apr 5-7	Finding Forrester	,,
Apr 12-21	Crazy for You	HAODS
Apr 24-28	The Best Little Whorehouse In Texas	Upstage Productions
Apr 30/May 2	Crouching Tiger, Hidden Dragon	Cinema
May 3-5	The Gift	,,
May 6	Voice and Characterisation Workshop	John Abbot
May 8-12	Thirtieth Kenton Drama Festival	
May 15-19	Miss Julie	Mr Armstrong
May 31/Jun 2	Spellbound	Organised Chaos Theatre Association
Jun 5-9	Calamity Jane	Woodley Light Operatic Society
Jun 11-13	Memento	Cinema
Jun 14-16	State and Main	,,
Jun 20-23	The End of the Pier Variety Show	Behind U Productions
Jun 28	The Angelettes	A Productions
Jun 29	An Evening with the Cellorhymics	Goring Gap Jazz Appreciation Society
Jul 15	Popstars	The Harlequin School of Dance
Jul 20-21	Summer Show	The Harlequin School of Dance
Oct 6	Silver Threads	Mike Hurst and his Little Band
Oct 16-20	Hay Fever	The Henley Players
Oct 22-24	Under the Sand	Cinema
Oct 25-27	Final Fantasy	,,
Oct 29-31	The Dish	,,
Nov 1-3	Lucky Break	,,
Nov 4-8	American Sweetheart	,,
Nov 9-10	When Brendan met Trudy	,,
Nov 16-24	Kiss Me Kate	HAODS
Nov 27/Dec 1	The Gondoliers	Woodley Light Operatic Society
Dec 4-8	Sweeney Todd	Henley College
Dec 9, 11, 13, & 14	Hansel and Gretel	English Pocket Opera
Dec 15-18	Joe Brown with His Bruvvers	
Dec 17-19	Croupier	Cinema
Dec 20-21	Lucky Break	,,
Dec 22	Carry On Gilbert and Sullivan	Opera Anywhere
Dec 31	Cinderella	Henley Children's Theatre Group

2002   The Kenton Theatre

Date	Event	Company
Jan 5	Cinderella	Henley Children's Theatre Group
Jan 14-16	The Others	Cinema
Jan 21-23	Bandits	,,
Jan 27	An Evening of Dance 2002	Harlequin School of Dance

Jan 28-29	Zoolander	Cinema
Feb 1-2	Step On! Into the Seventies	EJ Productions
Feb 6-9	Treasure Island	Behind U Productions
Feb 11-13	The 51st State	Cinema
Feb 14-16	Moulin Rouge	''
Feb 25/Mar 2	Rebecca	HAODS
Mar 5-9	Bells are Ringing	Masquerade Musical Theatre
Mar 10-16	Henley Youth Festival	
Mar 25-30	The Hothouse	The Henley Players
Apr 2-3	Butterfly's Tongue	Cinema
Apr 4-6	Mulholland Drive	''
Apr 9	Mozart by Candlelight	Dreammakers Ltd
Apr 13	London Pride	New London Entertainment
Apr 19-27	The Merry Widow	HAODS
Apr 28	The Magic Flute	Oxford Touring Opera
Apr 29/May 1	Kandahar	Cinema
May 2-4	K-Pax	''
May 5	Stage Technique and Acting Skills Workshop	Andrew Neil
May 7-11	Thirty-first Kenton Drama Festival	
May 20-25	Under Milk Wood	KT Productions
May 29/Jun 1	A Jubilee Variety Show	Behind U Productions
Jun 6-8	Not Peter	Organised Chaos Theatre Association
Jun 11-15	Me and My Girl	Woodley Light Operatic Society
Jun 16	Junior Star for a Night	Stageworks
Jun 17-18	La Veuve de Saint-Pierre	Cinema
Jun 19-20	In the Bedroom	''
Jun 21-22	Last Orders	''
Jun 23	Summer Review	Henley Children's Theatre Group
Jul 19-20	More About Dance	Harlequin School of Dance
Sep 21	Silver Threads	Mike Hurst and his Little Big Band
Oct 15-19	Confusions	The Henley Players
Oct 25/Nov 2	Oklahoma!	Henley Amateur Operatic
Nov 11-16	Inspector Drake and the Perfekt Crime	KT Productions
Nov 22-23	Amadeus the Director's Cut	Cinema
Nov 26-30	Patience	Woodley Light Operatic Society
Dec 6-7	Variety Showcase 2002	Stageworks
Dec 9-13	Two Men Went to War	Cinema
Dec 9	Before Film Meet Kenneth Cranham	
Dec 14-15	Joe Brown with Special Guests – The Bruvvers	
Dec 30/Jan 4	Aladdin	Henley Children's Theatre Group

2003 The Kenton Theatre

Jan 10-11	Tom, Dusty and Me	Mike Hurst presents
Jan 14-18	The Adventures of Robin Hood	Behind You Productions
Jan 24-25	Step On! Hollywood	EJ's Productions
Jan 26	An Evening of Dance	Harlequin School of Dancing
Jan 27/Feb 1	Die Another Day	Cinema

Date	Event	Company
Feb 7-8	The Lion, the Witch and the Wardrobe	Masquerade Youth Theatre
Feb 10-11	Rabbit Proof Fence	Cinema
Feb 12-15	Changing Lanes	Cinema
Feb 24/Mar 1	The Beaux' Stratagem	HAODS
Mar 5	A Night at the Musicals	Reading Theatre College
Mar 8	More Mozart by Candlelight	Locrian Ensemble
Mar 18-22	Move Over, Mrs Markham	The Henley Players
Mar 23-29	The Henley Youth Festival	
Apr 4-12	The Pirates of Penzance	HAODS
Apr 23	The Easter Holiday Show with Mr Chris	
Apr 24/May 10	The Kenton Film Festival	
May 11	Acting Shakespeare Workshop	Clifford Milner
May 14-17	Thirty-second Kenton Drama Festival	
Jun 3-7	Summer Madness	Behind You Productions
Jun 10-14	South Pacific	Woodley Light Operatic Society
Jun 15	Junior Star for a Night	Stageworks
Jun 16-17	Turn Your Radio On	Henley Childrens Theatre Group
Jun 23-28	Dial M for Murder	Black Widows
Jul 11-12	Dance 2 the Max	Harlequin School of Dancing
Jul 15-17	Bugsy Malone	St Mary's School
Sep 28	Kenton Theatre Friends Reception and Revue	
Oct 14-18	A Streetcar Named Desire	The Henley Players
Oct 21-25	The Blue Room	Orpheus Productions
Oct 30/Nov 1	The Wind in the Willows	Masquerade Youth Theatre
Nov 2	Hot Show Shuffle	
Nov 3-8	The League of Extraordinary Gentlemen	Cinema
Nov 14-22	Singin' in the Rain	HAODS
Nov 25-29	Trial by Jury and HMS Pinafore	Woodley Light Operatic Society
Nov 30	A Variety Show	Mo's Senior Stage School
Dec 4	An Evening of Clairvoyance and Mediumship	Stephen Holbrook
Dec 6-7	The Mike Hurst Christmas Show	Mike Hurst
Dec 10-12	A Christmas Showcase Spectacular	Stageworks
Dec 13-14	Joe Brown and his Bruvvers	
Dec 18	Christmas at the Kenton	
Dec 19-20	Puss in Boots	The Hurst Family
Dec 21-22	Peter Pan	Mo's Pantomime Company
Dec 30/Jan 3	Jack and the Beanstalk	Henley Children's Theatre Group

2004 The Kenton Theatre

Date	Event	Company
Jan 5-7	Calendar Girls	Cinema
Jan 8-10	Holes	Cinema
Jan 14-17	Sleeping Beauty	Behind You Productions
Jan 18	An Evening of Dance	Harlequin School of Dancing
Jan 21	Youth Speaks	Henley Rotary Club
Jan 30-31	Step On! Rock n' Pop	EJ's Productions
Feb 2-4	Kill Bill	Cinema

Feb 5-7	Master and Commander: The Far Side of the World	Cinema
Feb 12-14	A Night at the Music Hall	Kenton Theatre
Feb 15	An Evening with Gyles Brandreth	Henley Festival
Feb 16-17	In America	Cinema
Feb 18-19	Secondhand Lions	Cinema
Feb 20-21	Pirates of the Carribean: The Curse of the Black Pearl	Cinema
Feb 23-24	Seabiscuit	Cinema
Feb 25-26	Cold Mountain	Cinema
Feb 27	Vivaldi by Candlelight	Locrian Ensemble
Feb 28	Joe Brown and his Bruvvers	
Mar 2-6	Godspell	Masquerade Musical Theatre Co
Mar 16-20	The Playboy of the Western World	The Henley Players
Mar 22-27	The Henley Youth Festival	
Mar 28-29	Shirley Valentine	Cinema
Apr 1-3	Popcorn	Cinema
Apr 5-6	Girl with a Pearl Earring	Cinema
Apr 7-8	The Lord of the Rings: The Return of the King	Cinema
Apr 16-24	Jesus Christ Superstar	HAODS
Apr 25	The BBO Big Band	
Apr 26-28	The Last Samurai	Cinema
Apr 29/May 1	Three Men in a Boat	Rodney Bewes
May 2	Friendly Opera	Elsewhere Theatre Productions
May 6	The Caretaker	Blackeyed Theatre
May 9	Theatre Imagery Workshop	Mike Rogers
May 11-15	Thirty-third Kenton Drama Festival	
May 26-29	The Wiz	Behind You Productions
Jun 6-12	Half a Sixpence	Woodley Light Operatic Society
Jun 13	Junior Star for a Night	Stageworks
Sep 19	A Musical Revue	Kenton Theatre
Sep 25	The Gershwin Years	Tony Jacobs
Oct 5-9	The Winslow Boy	The Henley Players
Oct 11-13	The Notebook	Cinema
Oct 14-16	Stage Beauty	Cinema
Oct 18-20	Japanese Story	Cinema
Oct 21	Mad About Musicals	Madabout Productions
Oct 23	An Evening of Clairvoyance	Stephen Holbrook
Oct 28-30	Tin Pan Ali	Masquerade Stage School
Nov 1	Julian Lloyd Webber – Bossa Nova	Henley Festival Extra
Nov 2	Stacey Kent	,,
Nov 3	Fado with Ann Sophia Varela	,,
Nov 4	Collins and Read and Dimension	,,
Nov 5	Rainer Hersch and Rebecca Carrington	,,
Nov 6	Kit and the Widow	,,
Nov 14-20	Billy – The Musical	HAODS
Nov 23-27	The Yeomen of the Guard	Woodley Light Operatic Society
Nov 28	From Basin Street to Broadway	Keith Smith's Hefty Jazz
Dec 5	Domino's Magic Show	Kenton Theatre
Dec 8-9	A Christmas Showcase	Stageworks
Dec 10-11	Pride and Prejudice	Cinema

Dec 13-14	*Wimbledon*	Cinema
Dec 15-16	*Inside I'm Dancing*	Cinema
Dec 17-19	Joe Brown	Joe Brown Productions
Dec 26/Jan 1	*Babes in the Wood*	Henley Children's Theatre Group

2005 — The Kenton Theatre

Jan 3-4	*The Terminal*	Cinema
Jan 5-6	*Collateral*	Cinema
Jan 7-8	Mike Hurst	Mike Hurst
Jan 13-14	*I Heart Huckabees*	Cinema
Jan 15	*Abbey Road*	Waterloo Productions
Jan 24	Youth Speaks	Henley Rotary Club
Jan 28-29	*Garden State*	Cinema
Jan 30	An Evening of Dance	Dance Connections
Jan 31	*Before Sunrise*	Cinema
Feb 1	*Before Sunset*	Cinema
Feb 2	*Before Sunrise + Before Sunset*	Cinema
Feb 4	*Hittin' the Highspots*	Joe Brown
Feb 5	Rogers and Hammerstein Concert	Guildford Opera Company
Feb 6-12	*The Importance of Being Earnest*	Black Widows
Feb 27/Mar 12	*My Cousin Rachel*	The Henley Players
Mar 13-19	The Henley Youth Festival	
Mar 20	Big Band	
Apr 1	*Tribute to Queen*	John Holmes
Apr 2	Private Function	Rotary Club
Apr 3-9	*Alarms and Excursions*	Mirror Mirror
Apr 6	The Haunted Castle Show (11am & 2.15pm)	
Apr 10-23	*Oliver*	HAODS
Apr 29/May 7	*Les Miserables* (Youth Production)	KT Productions
May 7-14	Thirty-fourth Kenton Drama Festival	
May 15	Acker Bilk	Keith Smith
May 22-28		Behind You Productions
Jun 4	CWM Male Choir	HAODS
Jun 5-11	*Anything Goes*	Woodley Light Operatic Society
Jun 12	*Junior Star for a Night*	Stageworks
Jun 16-17	*Mad About Musicals*	
Jun 23	*Ancestral Voices*	Moray Watson
Jun 30	*The Gershwin Years*	Tony Jacobs
Jul 5	*Just a Minute*	BBC Recording
Jul 10-16	An Evening of Dance	Dance Connection
Sep 18/Oct 1	*Happy as a Sandbag*	HAODS
Oct 2-15	*Humble Boy*	The Henley Players
Oct 16-22	Festival Extra	Henley Festival
Oct 30/Nov 8	*School of Reform*	Kenton Theatre Bi-centenary

All associated with our well-trod stage...

Clive Merrison	Barry Howard	John Inman
 Richard Todd	Simon Williams	
Christopher Cazenove	Diana Rigg	Ed Stewart
Kate Winslet	Melvyn Hayes	Sheila Steafel
Geoffrey Durham	Rodney Bewes	Lionel Thomson
Harry Fowler	Roberta Nelson	Moray Watson

Celebrities who appeared at the Kenton

Albert Chevalier   Jun 1900   Variety
Music hall artist.   Jul 1901
Wrote and sang *My Old Dutch*.

Patrick Hamilton   Feb 1940   Directed *Gaslight*
Author and director.

Michael Gough   Oct 1944   *Old Acquaintance*
Actor, film and television.

Walter Gotell   May 1945   *Anna Christie*
Actor, film and television.

Sarah Churchill   Dec 1945   *Squaring the Triangle*
Actress.
Daughter of Winston Churchill.

William Franklin   Dec 1945   *Squaring the Triangle*
Actor, radio and television.

Pamela Hayes   Dec 1945   *Squaring the Triangle*
Actress, radio and television.

Alfred Burke   Oct 1946   *Dangerous Corner*
Actor, mainly television.

Rona Anderson   Jan 1947   *Beauty and the Beast*
Mrs Gordon Jackson.
Scottish film actress.

Adrian Stanley   May 1950   *Blithe Spirit*
Stage actor and director.

Dorothy Holmes-Gore   May 1950   *Blithe Spirit*
Actress mainly known for   Nov 1950   *The Foolish Gentlewoman*
her radio work.

Lana Morris   Jun 1950   *Young Wives Tale*
Popular film actress of the 50s.
Appeared in many Norman Wisdom films.

Ronald Howard   Jul 1950   *French Without Tears*
Post-war actor.
Son of Leslie Howard.

Carol Marsh   Jul 1950   *Yes and No*

Michael Medwin   Jul 1950   *The Man from the Ministry*
Television and film actor.
Later producer and director.

Sonia Holm   Jul 1950   *The Shining Hour*
               Dec 1950   *A Soldier for Christmas*

Diana Dors   Aug 1950   *Born Yesterday*
Popular film actress and beauty.
One of the *Rank Starlets*.

John Bentley   Sep 1950   *Ten Little Niggers*
Actor.
Famous as *Dick Barton, Special Agent*.

Avis Scott   Sep 1950   *Fools Rush In*
Popular stage actress of the
50s and 60s.

Barbara Murray Still acting today. One of the *Rank Starlets*.	Sep 1950 Dec 1950	*Miranda* *Mary Rose*	
Dinah Sheridan Film actress and later television. Best known for *Genevieve*.	Sep 1950	*Why Men Leave Home*	
Anthony Newley Stage and film actor and singer. Best known for *Stop the World I want to get off*.	Sep 1950	*Heaven and Charing Cross*	
Doris Hare Well known stage and revue actress.	Oct 1950	*Easy Money*	
Patricia Plunkett Well known repertory actress.	Oct 1950	*Claudia, Claudia*	
Hector Ross Repertory actor.	Oct 1950	*The Man in Possession*	
Kathleen Byron	Nov 1950	*Private Lives*	
John Marquand	Nov 1950	*The Ghost Train*	
Jane Hylton	Nov 1950	*The Eagle Has Two Heads*	
Patrick Holt Stage and film actor.	Dec 1950	*A Soldier for Christmas*	
Stanley McMurtry *Mac*. Cartoonist of the *Daily Mail*.	1959/60	Various Henley Players Productions	
Stephen Potter Author of the *Gamesmanship* books	1960	Kenton Arts Club	

Clive Merrison Television actor. Many parts including *Sherlock Holmes*.	1960's	Repertory	
Muir Mathieson Composer and conductor – especially of film music.	1961	Kenton Arts Club	
Dennis Matthews Concert pianist.	Apr 1967	Henley Concerts	
Eithne Dunn	Apr 1967	*Dear Liar*	
John Heddle Nash Well-known light tenor. Son of Heddle Nash.	May 1967	*Gilbert & Sullivan*	
Barry Howard Comic television and stage actor. Best known for *Hi-de-Hi*.	May 1967	*Job for the Boy*	
John Inman Comic television and stage actor. Best known for *Are You Being Served*.	May 1967	*Job for the Boy*	
Celia Johnson Classical actress, stage and film. Lived locally.	Jun 1967	*As the Poet Sees it*	
Michael MacLiammoir Well known as actor/manager at the Abbey Theatre, Dublin.	Jun 1967	*The Importance of Being Oscar*	
Richard Todd Well-known film and stage actor. Many films including *A Man Called Peter*.	Jun 1967	*As the Poet Sees It*	

Gladys Cooper Well-known classical actress. Lived locally.	Jun 1967	*As the Poet Sees It*
Tom Baker *Doctor Who*.	Jul 1967	*The Reluctant Debutante*
Simon Williams Actor and author. Best known for *Upstairs Downstairs*.	Jul 1967	*The Reluctant Debutante*
Margot Thomas Television actress mainly in long-running serials.	Jul 1967	*The Reluctant Debutante*
Diz Disley Jazz musician.	Jun 1968	Folk Entertainment
Nell Dunn Authoress. Best known for *Up the Junction*.	Mar 1973	Lecture
Cyril Fletcher Variety comedian and actor. Known for his *Odd Odes*.	Mar 1974	One Man Show
Christopher Cazenove Film and stage actor. Known for the *Colditz Story*.	Oct 1977	*Dummy Run*
Anthony Roye Television actor.	Feb 1978	*The Editor Regrets* Premier of WD Hume play
Denys Hawthorne *Dr Mays* in *Within these Walls*.	Feb 1978	*The Editor Regrets*
Marsha Fitzalan Film and television star.	Feb 1978	*The Editor Regrets*
Frank Williams Actor. The Vicar in *Dad's Army*.	Feb 1978	*The Editor Regrets*
Diana Rigg Actress in film and television. Known for *The Avengers*.	1978	*With Great Pleasure* (Recorded)
Roy Hudd Stand up comedian and comic actor.	1979	*Roy Hudd's Music Hall*
Mary Hopkin Popular singer.	Mar 1980	*Victorian Extravaganza*
Vince Hill Popular singer and entertainer.	1981	*An Evening with Vince Hill*
Ed Stewart (Stewpot) Children's TV presenter.	1981	*An Evening with Vince Hill*
Roger de Courcey Ventriloquist with *Nookie Bear*.	1981	*An Evening with Vince Hill*
George Chisholm Well-known jazz trombonist and comedian.	1981	*Keith Smith's Jazz*
Melvyn Hayes Actor – *Ain't half hot, mum*.	Apr 1982	Stage Struck
John Junkin Comedian, actor, writer.	Nov 1982	*One Portion Sweet and Sour Ham*

Sheila Steafel Actress/comedienne – *The Frost Report*.	1983	*One Woman Show*
Raymond Baxter Television personality.	1985	*Save the Regal Campaign*
Geoffrey Durham *The Great Soprendo*.	1985	*Magic Show*
Lucy Fleming Mrs Simon Williams – actress.	1985	*Save the Regal Campaign*
Jenny Hanley Actress and children's TV presenter.	1985	*Save the Regal Campaign*
Sheridan Morley Author etc.	1985	*Save the Regal Campaign*
Robert Morley Actor.	1985	*Save the Regal Campaign*
Guy Siner Actor – *Hello, hello*.	1985	*Save the Regal Campaign*
Ian Partridge Tenor.	1985	*Henley Concerts*
John Mortimer Barrister, author.	1986	*Mortimer's Miscellany*
Constance Cummings Actress.	1986	*Fanny Kemble at Home*
Sylvia Sims Lady Attenburgh – actress.	1988	*A Summer in the South*
Jeremy Irons Actor. Introduced the film *The Dressmaker*.	1989	*Midnight matinee*
Joe Brown Popular singer (with the *Bruvvers*).	1990's	*Various Christmas Shows*
Kate Winslet Actress mainly in films like *The Titanic*. Lived locally.	1991	*The Secret Diary of Adrian Mole*
Kenneth Cranham Well-known film and television actor.	2002	*Introduced Two Men went to War*
Rodney Bewes One of the *Likely Lads*.	May 2004	*Three Men in a Boat*
Frankie Vaughan Was attending a pantomime production and was invited to sing!!!		
Moray Watson Actor.	2005	*One Man Show*